Unexpected Lessons

from Professor Higgins

By
Patti Smith

Dedicated to those willing to view unexpected challenges as lessons for transformation.

CURRICULUM

PREREQUISITES

UNDERGRADUATE COURSES

MASTER'S COURSES

DOCTORATE COURSES

WORK/LIFE EXPERIENCE

PREREQUISITES

LESSON 1

One Lucky Student

There is an old adage which claims, "When the student is ready, the teacher will appear." That is *not* what happened to me. I was neither prepared nor ready when my greatest teacher appeared.

It was the late 1970's and I was just twenty-one when our family doctor apologized as he diagnosed my newborn with Down syndrome. The doctor's face and voice were full of pity when he suggested I place my son in an institution. But I knew I never would. One look into my baby boy's tender, blue/grey eyes and I was hooked.

The doctor's diagnosis dazed me. As a naïve, undaunted newlywed armed solely with a "happily ever after" mind set, I had previously only seen myself cheerfully riding the wave of the American Dream—believing my future children and I could have or accomplish any goal we sought—if we simply worked hard enough.

Instead of excitement over my new baby boy, I initially received merely sympathy from family and friends. Until I learned to stop listening to medical experts, I heard only discouraging, pessimistic feedback from doctors with no expectations for my son to live to adulthood or accomplish anything.

My husband handled his feelings stoically and privately. If he was sad or worried, I never knew. He listened to me vent my feelings and concerns without criticism or any negative comments, but he rarely spoke about our son's medical conditions or his future.

It seemed as if a heavy curtain had dropped on me, symbolizing the final scenes of my youth. But instead of receiving the support and praise I'd expected for raising a perfect child, I felt alone on a stage in an empty auditorium, facing only dense silence oozing with fear of the unknown. Little did I know at the time—I had no idea there was so much for me to learn—I'd one day realize how perfect my son really was. He was perfect for me.

As I rocked my baby and held him tightly in my arms, determination surged through me. I believed the might of my love and strength could be enough to protect him, and I would dedicate my life to teaching and raising my gentle, quiet child.

But I was wrong! To my amazement and delight, it has been my son who spent his life teaching me instead. And it's been an entertaining, adventurous and exhilarating ride! His teachings changed me from a young woman who was scared and overwhelmed by the diagnosis of Down syndrome to a mother who considers having such a child as marvelous as receiving a bouquet of four-leaf clovers.

Even more than just being lucky, it has been my experience that having a child with Down syndrome has felt as if I were gifted with a golden key which opened doors to unique experiences offering profound enlightenment. And I'm confident I wouldn't have learned these lessons as well through conventional education.

Throughout my son's life—even into his twenties—a few friends and extended family members have asked me how I raised my son in such a manner that he seemed so happy and content. Also, why did our family appear extraordinarily cheerful and unphased by any challenges presented by my son's diagnosis?

Their questions always caught me off guard because my family had nothing to be "phased" about. Why wouldn't we be happy? Most who asked were older—from a different generation when institutions were prevalently used to house those with mental issues. Perhaps they didn't understand how delightful it is to have a child with Down syndrome in our family and how much we've enjoyed the unexpected, unusual and exceptional experiences he presented. This book will address those questions and reveal how my son, Christopher Higgins, became the happiness super glue in out family.

Even though I gave it my all, I'm not the reason for Christopher's success or his positive effect on others. The only thing I congratulate myself for is my willingness to remain a student—to learn from my son—and my openness to transform. Because of my immense love for him and desire to support his happiness, I chose to be open and curious at opportune times and learn from him rather than needing to be right or appear smarter than I am.

My son is forty-five at the time of this writing and I'm not sure I deserve credit for having taught him anything. He's still as remarkable and stubbornly unique as when he was a young child who seemed disinterested in learning to walk or talk for way too long. And the good news is—I've learned more from him than he has from me.

It took years, but eventually young Christopher hit all the physical developmental milestones. He learned to walk and talk—in his own unique ways. He has always decided what he learns and when. Ah ha! One of my early and essential life lessons—we each evolve in our own time, and in our own ways. When the student is willing to receive, teaching can happen. However, actual enlightenment and growth do not occur unless the student chooses to learn. My son taught me how futile it is to resent or disrespect the timing of personal growth in others.

These are the reasons why I respectfully refer to Christopher as my own Professor Higgins. (The name is the same as the main character in *Pygmalion* written by George Bernard Shaw (1912) which later became the movie *My Fair Lady* (1964). Although my Professor Higgins is neither a misogynist nor an elitist, he is a bit unconventional and actually quite loverly.)

While I'm still a work in progress and don't hold myself out as a brilliant student, it's my privilege to share Professor Higgins' stories and how he taught me to see life through an extraordinary lens. From unusual and often stunning lessons, I learned how much joy there can be in

letting go—surrendering—my own fallible beliefs and expectations. I discovered happiness and peace in acceptance, to anticipate that great opportunities may arise when leaning in to the unexpected, and how to free myself from some fears. These lessons allowed opportunities to have fun during unplanned moments of life and enjoy the ultimate journey of the way my life turned out.

Before reading further, a few disclaimers are warranted. First, this is *not* a parenting book on how to face and overcome a perceived challenge such as raising a child with unique needs. I don't pretend to be an expert qualified to render parenting advice. Rather, many of the lessons shared in this book come from my mistakes. Indeed, I've been more than lucky to have gleaned new perspectives, wisdom and abundant happiness from many unpredictable and amusing experiences.

Secondly, it is important to understand that although many children and adults with Down syndrome have some traits or physical features in common, these individuals are *not* the same. These beautiful people are vibrant in their selfhood and clearly are not clones of each other. What I've learned from Professor Higgins might not mirror what others in similar circumstances have learned.

Finally, it isn't my intent to gloss over any challenges of raising a child with Trisomy 21. Rather, I seek to explain how the marvelous joy, wisdom and knowledge which I've received have far outweighed the hardships.

The most universal lesson my son has taught me is that profound teachings abound through all of life's experiences, whether easy or hard, good or bad. Looking

retrospectively at the path my life has taken, I can readily see that my maximum growth happened at times of opposition. The more difficult the challenge or the more unexpected the event, the greater the opportunity for learning and refinement.

I wrote this book for the parent who is seeking to find the joy in their struggle, or who hasn't yet found silver linings to challenges, and for anyone who desires to be inspired by stories of triumph and who choses joy.

This book is dedicated to my son, Professor Higgins, who raised my awareness not only about how to love and enjoy life with him, but also about improving my interactions with all of humanity. Some people may call him "severely disabled," some may refer to him as "handicapped," or others may even use the technical medical term of "severely mentally retarded."[1] But none of those terms seem fitting to me.

I simply and gratefully call him my beloved son and master teacher.

---

[1] Mental retardation became a medical term in the 19th century and is still used as a legal term to describe people with intellectual disabilities. Because "the R-word" has become used as an epithet or derogatory term in our society, it is widely considered to be a slur and is especially offensive and searing to those who have the diagnosis or love a person with Down syndrome. Significant progress to ameliorate this issue occurred in 2010 when federal law required the U.S. government to update its language from "mental retardation" to "intellectual disability" (Rosa's Law, as codified in Public Law 111–256). Soon afterwards, the change was also adopted by the American Psychiatric Association in its Diagnostic and Statistical Manual for Mental Disorders (DSM-5).

LESSON 2

Meeting Professor Higgins

I t was bound to be a wonderful day. I had been looking forward to this day for almost nine months and I was finally getting ready to leave the hospital with my new baby—two days after his birth. While waiting for the nurse to bring my baby from the nursery, I happily laid out his travel clothes—a darling newborn-sized blue and white sailor outfit with white hat and booties—which had been carefully selected weeks before. I sat next to my bed and wondered what was taking the nurses so long to bring my baby to my room. But I knew I needed to be patient because things often took longer in a hospital on a military base.

When the door opened, I was surprised to see our doctor and nurse walk in with another nurse I didn't recognize. Our usual nurse was pushing sleeping Christopher in the wheeled hospital bassinette. I grinned at the very sight of my baby.

"Oh, how nice! I didn't expect a farewell party!" I

teased. "You have been so great to us." He wasn't just our family doctor; he was also a friend of the family we knew through church. Having his extra kindness and care had really made our birth experience much nicer than what I had expected in a military hospital.

"Just one last check to see how you're feeling," our doctor said. My nurse rolled baby Christopher next to me as the new nurse stepped back and stood next to the door.

"I'm fine. Thanks for checking on me. I'm just relieved to finally be going home." I smiled and leaned over the bassinette for a closer look at my adorable baby boy. Ahhh, my heart melted with his scent—like a mixture of soap and fresh bread.

"We're happy you're going home too," the doctor said. "But before you leave, we think there's one more test we'd like to do."

"For me or my son?"

"Your son is being tested for Down syndrome." The doctor's voice was matter-of-fact, practically sterile. "We aren't sure..." he added, shaking his head slightly back and forth. "In fact, I don't think your baby has this condition—he doesn't look as if he does—but one of the nurses thinks it's a possibility. So, a blood test is recommended to rule it out."

I'd never heard of whatever that "down" condition was and didn't worry since the doctor sounded so cavalier and I trusted his wisdom. I certainly didn't know to ask why or look for physical markers. I picked up my tiny six-pound

newborn and cradled him without much thought about the test. I was already in love with my perfect baby.

"If you need my consent and you think it's a good idea, then sure, please go ahead," I replied.

"The blood sample needs to be sent to the lab in San Diego for testing, so we don't expect results for several weeks." Our doctor's voice remained gentle but impassive. "Do you have any questions?"

"No, not really." I stammered. Because our doctor didn't seem concerned about whatever Down syndrome was and there appeared to be no rush to receive the lab results, I figured the testing was merely routine. It was my first baby—what did I know? I shook off his comments, thanked him for going out of his way and giving us this extra care, and said good-bye.

Our nurse rolled Christopher back to the nursery and returned with him a brief time later. I was relieved he wasn't crying and assumed the test had been simple. I was more concerned that his newborn outfit was way too big for him and covered half of his face. Awashed by his charm I smiled and scolded him in baby talk for being so tiny. After he was dressed in his darling travel clothes, I cuddled him in my arms and admired everything about him. I was excited to take him home and place him in our freshly painted and decorated nursery. I was euphorically happy and didn't even feel the need to say anything about the recommended extra test to my husband.

I almost forgot all about it.

But the grave look on the face of that new nurse who lingered at the back of my hospital room during that discharge conversation haunted my memory, causing the unknown test results to linger in the back of my mind. Eventually, my curiosity was piqued enough to motivate me to investigate the condition. I reasoned that I should at least know something about the condition which the test was supposed to "rule out" before mentioning anything about it to my husband or parents.

Having never heard of Down syndrome before, I began my research by rummaging through my mother's bookshelves. One of my favorite things about my mom was her love for learning. Her collection of encyclopedias, dictionaries and reference books filled most of her bookcases. In an old medical reference book, I discovered Down syndrome to be the name of a genetic disorder which occurs during gestation. It is reportedly caused when abnormal cell division results in extra genetic material in Chromosome 21 of every cell in the body. That description seemed fairly innocuous, but then I was alarmed to learn that in most cases the effect of this little chromosome duplication is severe developmental and intellectual delays.

Aaah! Although that information astounded me, it also didn't make sense. Wouldn't the doctor have appeared more concerned if they were testing my baby for this sort of serious condition? I was dumbfounded. But the more I read, the more certain I became that this diagnosis definitely couldn't apply to my perfect, beautiful baby. He was a little bit of a sleepy head, to be sure, and fairly mellow. But he wasn't....he didn't look like he had any mental problems. And, that sort of problem certainly wouldn't happen *to me*.

Because of our acquaintance through church activities, I trusted that our doctor sincerely cared about my little family and would have said more if he genuinely thought the diagnosis of Down syndrome could be legitimate. And I distinctly remembered him saying he didn't think it was probable and that the test results would just confirm his belief.

My baby was fine. He just had to be!

When reviewing the hospital scene in my mind's eye, and seeing the doctor's unconcerned, peaceful demeanor, I could also see the solemn look on the face of that new nurse standing in the back of the room, with her eyes intently focused on the doctor and then on me. I started to realize that she looked concerned. She must have been the one who questioned it—perhaps that was why she was there.

My confusion eventually prompted a quick trip to the city library where I could read from more current encyclopedias and medical books. (This is how research was done before the Internet.) I needed closure.

The librarian directed me to the Medical Reference section of the library. I pulled out the thickest, most official looking reference book I could find about general medical conditions. Under the topic of Down syndrome, I saw a black and white picture of a young man who appeared to be in his 20's—he didn't look like a kid, but also didn't look like an adult. The proportionate size of his head seemed off. Either his head was larger than usual, or his ears looked too small or positioned too low. He wasn't smiling but blankly stared straight at the camera. He looked like he was heavily medicated or completely unaware of what was going on around him. Even the shape of his eyes seemed unusual with somewhat of a flat appearance, and his tongue protruded from his slightly gaping mouth. Because his head was shaved and he was wearing a hospital gown I imagined he was living in an asylum for the mentally ill, abandoned by his family who were incapable of taking care of his serious medical needs. But the worst part of his image was a dark blotch covering a large part of his forehead and side of his head which looked like either a birthmark or a wound. I caught my breath, shuddered, and slammed the book shut. My baby looked nothing like that young man! Christopher was darling and charming. Whew! The nurse clearly had to be wrong. That picture ended any further curiosity or inquiry about the subject. This sort of tragedy could never happen to my son, not to my family and certainly not to me.

I had a lot to learn.

While awaiting test results during Christopher's first four weeks of life, I didn't worry further about him having any medical problems. He was a perfect, beautiful, easy baby who rarely cried.

Everything changed the day Christopher received a blessing in church. I sat in the church pew with my heart floating on a cloud of happiness as our sweet baby, clothed in white, was lifted by his father and held high for everyone to see—like the Simba pose in the Lion King. I glanced at our doctor sitting across the chapel, pleased by his proud smile.

I felt like a blushing bride hearing the "ohhhs" and "ahhhs" from my friends in the congregation. As the words of his father, who gave the blessing, echoed through the microphone, I hung onto every word. My husband spoke beautiful words from his heart. I smiled hearing the promise of good health and a happy life and breathed a quiet sigh of relief.

But I was surprised when I heard the promise, "when you die, your mission in life will be completed." Without delving too deeply into our church's doctrine, a life's mission is essentially one's unique purpose in life. Our church teaches that life is the time to live by faith and prepare to return home to God. Considering the importance of personal choice and agency in our church's teachings, it didn't sit well with me that Christopher was promised to successfully fulfill his mission in life without thought for his own choices. For example, what if my son didn't want to be a member of our church? I would support his right to choose. Since it didn't make sense, I quickly discounted that promise to be just his father's fanciful dreams for his son's future to turn out well.

After church we went to dinner at my parents' house because my father had been ill and had missed Christopher's blessing. As soon as we arrived my dad asked us to come to his room and tell him about the blessing. My husband related everything…almost.

"You left out one interesting part of the blessing," I said when he was done. "I heard you say when Christopher dies, his mission in life will be completed." They both eyed me quizzically as I continued, "but, I don't think that's a promise or blessing that could be given. Everybody has a personal mission in life and it's not in line with what our church teaches about the importance of individual agency regarding personal desires and choices for the direction of each person's life."

"Hmh, I don't remember that…and, I don't think I would have said that." My husband shook his head slowly.

After a few moments of silence, I frowned as I heard myself add, "The promise would only apply if someone was not accountable…" My words ended abruptly, and my eyes opened wide.

At that moment, I knew. I can't explain how or why, but the information download hit me as if the earth stopped in its rotation. I realized if Christopher were mentally impaired, he might not be held fully accountable by God for his choices in life. A diagnosis of Down syndrome could be fitting. My world would never be the same.

It was true. It was real and it was happening to me.

I walked, alone, out of my father's room toward the living room. I don't know if my husband followed me or was even nearby as I sat dazed on the piano bench. I can't recall how long I sat there and only remember my mother's voice snapping me out of my stupor when she announced that dinner was ready.

I was the only one who knew about the test and pending results. I hadn't mentioned it previously because I didn't genuinely believe there was anything to be concerned about. I had mistakenly trusted in our doctor's nonchalant demeanor on discharge day and the information in the reference books seemed wholly unbelievable. It didn't seem right to worry anyone needlessly. Sure, our baby was super mellow and rarely made sounds, but I didn't think anything was unusual—especially because I was so attentive to him.

As soon as I sat down at the table, however, I knew it was time.

It was the right moment to tell everyone about the pending test results. While my mom's fried chicken, corn and salad sat untouched on the dinner table I explained what I recalled from the doctor's discharge conversation and what little I'd read about Down syndrome. I didn't have the strength—or the heart—to describe that picture of the young man in the library's medical reference book. After my announcement, we all sat in uncomfortable silence. My husband ended the conversation with, "I guess we'll just have to wait for the test results."

"Yes, keep us informed as soon as you know·anything," my mom nodded.

I silently thought, "but, I *do* know." I was grateful for the discussion to end. I wasn't sure what my husband and parents thought about my news because everything seemed blurry, including their faces. Our baby slept comfortably in the next room as I sat quietly through dinner masking my emotions with an "everything will be fine" look on my face. I joined in their conversations pretending to be interested and contemplative, but inside I was sad, hopeless, angry and afraid all at the same time.

Nothing further was mentioned about Christopher's well-being for the rest of the day. Nobody dared.

I didn't sleep well for the next few nights. I didn't function well either. I was caught up in fear limbo— unable to understand and accept all the sweet feelings I had enjoyed over Christopher's first weeks of life and unable to face the pending test results or our future. I spent a lot of time just staring at my sweet, melancholy baby, constantly noting how he looked nothing like the young man pictured in that book. I reasoned that my imagination must have distorted the picture to have appeared scarier than it actually was.

Gratefully, a call came that same week inviting me to meet with a newly assigned pediatrician to receive the test results for our baby. My husband couldn't get time away from work, and I didn't protest. I was more comfortable handling tough situations by myself.

The next day I sat down in an examination room holding my tranquil baby tightly in my arms, as if I could protect my little Christopher from the weight of the expected news. I refused to let the world hurt my baby or crush our future.

The doctor walked in carrying only a thin, brown folder. He didn't smile as he greeted me and sat in a chair on the other side of the small room. I shifted in the hard chair suddenly cognizant of its pressure and moved my son from one arm to the other. As was Christopher's usual nature, he didn't fuss—he just looked at me with calm, trusting eyes. In a deliberate but gentle manner the doctor said, "The test results have come back. I'm sorry to tell you that your son has Trisomy 21, a condition commonly referred to as Down syndrome." He paused for only a moment before asking, "How much do you know about this diagnosis?"

"Ummm...not much." I immediately regretted not knowing more and allowing my fear to stop me when I slammed the book shut.

The doctor pulled out a single white sheet of paper, the entire contents of the folder, and handed it to me. "This is a printout of the test results."

I stared at the page and what looked like dozens of black jellybean shaped spots scattered across 4 horizontal black lines. The reality of the gravity of what I might be facing hit me—hard. The doctor's words became faint, jumbled and incoherent. They couldn't penetrate the wall of fear and confusion forming in my brain. I think he was explaining the diagnosis, but I felt like a student in a "Peanuts" reel with the teacher's voice sounding like, "wah…wah…wah."

I leaned toward the doctor and watched his mouth to better understand his words. "This is a copy of the genetic test which shows an extra chromosome on the 21st chromosome of every cell in your child's body. This result proves the diagnosis of Trisomy 21."

I looked down at the paper and noticed how the jellybean shapes were grouped in pairs. On the third horizontal line one group of dark spots was circled with red ink. All other groupings had two black spots, but the circled one had three. My mind was blank, and I couldn't speak.

I don't recall if the doctor continued his explanations or whether he waited for me to ask a question. A haze surrounded me, and I felt very alone with my baby. All I could think of was to count the pairs of black spots, which I did slowly, stopping at the red circle. *Maybe they made a mistake.* My eyes frantically scanned the paper looking for evidence of a mistake—someone else's name, the wrong date…anything.

Nothing appeared out of order, except for that offensive red ink circling those three jellybean silhouettes.

"And this is a picture of the 21st chromosome…with three?" I wanted to ask a poignant question but could only formulate the one.

As the doctor continued, I strained to focus on his words, hoping to remember them so I could relay them to my husband. "Trisomy 21 causes severe mental retardation."

I opened my mouth, but the doctor continued anticipating my question. "It's not a curable condition."

He paused and waited for me to say something, for what seemed to be an excruciatingly long time.

I drew in a deep breath and quickly exhaled. "What treatment is there? Ummm...how do I help him?" I mustered a fake smile to mask my doubt and appear confident.

"There is no treatment. We will need to monitor your son closely for medical problems associated with this diagnosis, such as heart defects and an autoimmune deficiency."

I had no words. *How could it be so hopeless?* The more the doctor spoke, the worse I felt. I'm not sure what else he said, but recall feeling my head moving involuntarily back and forth as if to say, "No." I wanted to say, "But we live in a modern world! There must be something we can do...and modern science...and..." But I said nothing.

The doctor continued his penetrating stare and softened his voice. "I'm sorry to tell you that your son's life expectancy is short. You should understand that he probably won't live past the age of seven."

My shoulders dropped as an audible sigh escaped my lungs. Each new piece of information the doctor added felt like a punch in the gut.

After another long pause the doctor said, "Some families elect to place children such as these in hospitals or institutions."

My head began again to shake, "No." The words, "children such as these" felt like poison inside me. I instinctively stood up to leave. I couldn't take any more. *An institution?* I looked down at my son who was quietly staring at me with his peaceful, angelic eyes. We knew each other well beyond his first six weeks of life. We had fallen in love with each other. No doctor, no diagnosis and especially no institution could break our bond and separate us.

I held my baby close to me with one arm and reached out with the other to shake the doctor's hand goodbye. Jumping to his feet, he grasped my hand. He tilted his head and smiled while still maintaining a concerned, furrowed brow, "I'm sure you need to think about this and will have many questions. You can call my office at any time. We'll be contacting you shortly to schedule more tests."

I hated his pity. It made me nauseous. I could barely utter, "thank you," as I moved quickly past him to push the door open. I hoped he couldn't see my tear-flooded eyes. My body walked out of the medical building that afternoon, but my head remained stuck in a haze. It was difficult to walk because I could barely see through my tears. Some flowed from sorrow, but most stemmed from fear and anger. I couldn't process everything I'd just heard—it seemed to not get past my filter of *"why me?"*

My darling baby boy didn't look slow or so sickly that he could die in seven short years! No way can his outlook be that grim and hopeless!

I sat in my car in the parking lot until I controlled my tears. I didn't call my husband right away or any family members. I processed it alone—I somehow felt I needed to be strong before sharing the news with others.

Intuitively I knew I needed to seek answers from somewhere else; the old encyclopedia and our doctors simply hadn't provided acceptable answers. I desperately needed positive information and was determined to find some. That spark of determination rose in me like flames and boiled away my tears. *I'd show that doctor how wrong he was—he just had to be!*

***

So began my tutelage with Christopher Higgins that summer of 1978. After wading through miserable news from doctors, medical journals and too many depressing articles, I finally resolved to stop reading any historical resources. I sought out only current information. I was steadfast in maintaining hope to find any positive news about my son's condition and chose to look forward instead of back at what I deemed to be ignorance of the past.

Eventually, I found encouragement and helpful advice from younger teachers and recently educated therapists. But the most optimistic news came from other parents in the Down syndrome community whom I met at conferences or in therapy sessions. They were also looking ahead with optimistic ideas and hopes for new possibilities in our children's futures. Every year Christopher grew older, it seemed the other parents and I held less trepidation and had more peace and happiness.

As I'd suspected—somewhere deep inside my soul, I'd known—much of the advice the doctor rendered in 1978 was antiquated or simply wrong.

Not only is there much better news today about the health and life expectancy of people diagnosed with Down syndrome, but also about capabilities and opportunities. Not just my son, but I've met many charming adults with this diagnosis who have lived well past their 40's and 50's. Through love and support from families and communities, the world of possibilities has and will continue to expand for these exceptional people.

Today, new parents welcome their children born with Down syndrome into a more optimistic world where they can experience unique depths of love, laughter, and joy which they might otherwise never have known, but for their remarkable child. And I believe that because of the support of good parents and caring societies, the bar for children with Down syndrome will continue to be raised.

Over my son's forty-five years—which I've never taken for granted—I've been delighted to witness many impressive possibilities for individuals with Down syndrome. I've personally met numerous articulate, exceptional men and women. Many have become national and international Special Olympic athletes, as well as successfully breaking barriers in other conventional sports including triathlons, swimming, and gymnastics. Some have testified to the United States Congress while others openly share opinions and ideas in public discourse about how society can support their success. Several have become Hollywood movie actors, social media influencers, entrepreneurs and volunteers in our communities. Multitudes have excelled well beyond prior educational and career expectations.

It has become the norm for men and women with this diagnosis to actively participate in planning for their futures and making important life decisions, including relationships and marriage. While a diagnosis of Down syndrome has proven not to be as limiting as previously thought, there is still much more to learn about the cause, ramifications and possibilities of Trisomy 21.

I don't pretend to intelligently speak about all people with Down syndrome, but I know my mentor. In my eyes, Christopher is as darling and loveable to me today as he was when I held him as a newborn in the doctor's office on that dreary day in 1978.

I'll never forget how my intuitive wisdom as a twenty-one year old mother gave me the strength to boldly walk out of the doctor's office when peppered with predictions of only pessimistic future outcomes for my child. Eventually, I learned that advice from doctors and other professionals was simply that—general advice, not direction.

Although my educational journey with Professor Higgins had a hard start, it turned into an adventurous, exhilarating trek through life with my son at my side. And I've become a much better person for having made the journey.

Early lessons taught by Professor Higgins laid an essential foundation for my ability to not only face challenges in life, but also to enjoy the breeze while sailing past them. In addition to understanding the importance of listening within, I also had to learn to trust myself and rely on my intuition, even when standing alone in my beliefs.

While I respect and appreciate any expert's particular knowledge, skills and competency, they aren't the ultimate decision makers for me or my family. I remain accountable and claim the authority to make medical and any important decisions based not only on expert advice, but also on my own gut instincts.

When I first met my son, I thought I would spend my life teaching him and worried I couldn't be the type of magnificent mother he needed me to be. Eventually, I was delighted to realize that we were both exactly who we needed each other to be.

Even from his early years, my son taught me one of the most significant universal truths—that the life of a child with Down syndrome is something to celebrate.

LESSON 3

I Don't Know What I Don't Know

On a hot August afternoon in southern California, my girlfriend, Cindy, and I sat by the side of the pool. It was only two weeks before Chris would be born; we were both twenty-one, both eight months pregnant and both expecting our first child. We commiserated about feeling as big as mother elephants. Unable to fit in swimsuits—or too embarrassed to try—we dangled our feet in the cool water as we sipped lemonade and shared dreams about motherhood.

Those were the days before ultrasounds and extravagant gender reveal parties. We knew nothing about our children soon to be born, hoping only for a healthy baby.

"I think I'm going to have a child with a handicap of some type." Cindy's words stunned me.

"Why would you say that?" I asked.

"I have an uncle with a mental disability, and he is so wonderful to be around. My grandparents take great care of him and everyone in the family adores him."

"Whoa," was all I could think of to say. She'd never mentioned her uncle before. I searched my brain for something positive to say but was speechless. I wanted to say, "I'm sorry," but Cindy's cheerful confidence made it seem awkward.

"I think I could do it," she continued. "I feel prepared to handle being the mother of a special baby who may need extra love."

"Better you than I!" My kind friend was easy to admire. She was nice to everyone, thought of others' needs and routinely looked for ways to be helpful.

I explained that I'd never known anyone with a mental challenge. I hoped I didn't sound too shallow—especially compared to Cindy's loving heart—but I was confident that I could never handle being the mother of such a child.

"Sometimes we can do more than we think we can," Cindy counseled.

"I don't know. I could never be as patient as you are, Cindy. I think you're amazing and will be a fantastic mother, even if your baby ends up having challenges or disabilities."

Christopher was born soon after with the eventual diagnosis of Down syndrome. Cindy's baby was born only a few weeks later, but without any syndrome, condition or diagnosis. You can bet I had a few conversations with God about my concerns and conundrum. Had God confused the two of us? Cindy was willing and ready to raise a child such as Christopher. I was clearly incapable.

Prior to this splintering point in my life, I had been optimistically on course to achieve ambitious goals I had set for myself and my future children. Getting pregnant as a twenty-year-old newlywed was a little inconvenient, but I vowed it wouldn't hinder my dreams to attend college, law school and eventually raise a family. I could do it all!

When I was a child, I'd imagined raising children to become significant players in the game of life and I looked forward to the adventure. My children would care about others, and lift humanity in such a way for the world to become a better place.

We were patriots; my husband was a distinguished United States Marine, and I envisioned our children being inspired by his heroic example. Living in the era of the Cold War and Vietnam, I vowed to teach my children to have a keen awareness of local and world-wide issues. This could be the generation to finally eradicate racism and usher in world peace. I didn't know exactly how I'd accomplish these ambitious objectives, but now my future seemed hazy. I hadn't anticipated needing to work with severe medical challenges. Certainly, any diagnosis of "intellectual delay" didn't fit into my vision for our future because those problems belonged to people in a train on a different track than the one on which I had been riding, which was traveling full steam ahead with no curves in sight.

Facing Christopher's medical diagnosis meant I had to look directly at those curves ahead. Initially, I grieved over the permanence and severity of our situation. I was told that it's going to be hard, but no one could explain exactly what the hardships would be. How would I prepare for unknown, but expected challenges? I felt as if I experienced more grief over the chaos of the unknown than I did about my son's diagnosis. I suffered needlessly because I didn't know enough about the truth of Trisomy 21. The only thing I was certain of was that I needed a plan.

As the daughter of a decorated United States Marine Corps Officer, I was taught throughout my life to always have a strategy and to reject – even abhor – the concept of surrender. Quitting was never an option. Failure was not an acceptable outcome. Rather, I was raised to establish goals with strategies and timelines to achieve them. If I wanted something badly enough and was willing to work hard enough, I knew I could accomplish anything—Oorah!

Before I could develop a realistic plan, however, I needed more information about...well, everything. I had previously stopped researching Down syndrome because I couldn't find any positive details. I had reasoned that it was preferable to be uninformed and for my mind to remain empty rather than filled with gunk. But I didn't know where to find hopeful information.

Purposeful ignorance was a foreign concept to me, but the old, overwhelming pessimistic information had sabotaged my ability to plan for or envision our future. What goals could reasonably be set for my son? These first months were my darkest season with Christopher. I was confused and I didn't know what I didn't know.

One day, when my baby was about three months old, I looked in the mirror and said, "you're such a bad choice to be Christopher's mother." I looked in my sparkling brown eyes so full of ambition and for the first time thought, "You can't reconcile who you are and what Christopher needs." I was a compulsive achiever who measured success more by tangible results than by comfort and happiness. I'd never met anyone with a mental disability or seen someone raise a child with one. My eyes filled with tears of self-pity and confusion. "*How are you going to raise this child?*" Before this pivotal moment, I hadn't seen obstacles as opportunities for learning and changing but considered them merely as hurdles to get over—the faster the better. I was in unknown territory without a map or itinerary.

Initially, the more I tried to envision Christopher's future, the more fear I had. Would his childhood look like mine? Would my son ever have friends? Would he even be invited to parties or participate in team sports? My heart hurt as I pictured Christopher as a lonely teenager standing on the sideline of a basketball court never being picked for a team or included in the fun. How could I make sure my child would be a success and have a happy life?

I might not have known how to be Christopher's mother, but the one thing I did know, was how much I hated the looks of pity my son and I received at church or in other social groups. The word had apparently spread quickly through my friends' circles but very few spoke with me directly about my son's diagnosis. I interpreted their condolences as unfair assessments of my son's future capabilities—and mine also! I wasn't fully convinced that Chris' life was sad news.

But their silence frustrated me more. It was hurtful and didn't seem right when people gushed and admired other babies in the room who were near my son's age but stammered when speaking to me. I tried to ignore the secreted stares and times when people abruptly turned away from making eye contact with me. Noticing some people intentionally looking away—pretending Christopher wasn't there—hurt the worst and made me angry. It motivated me to do all I could to make sure my son would not live a life of invisibility.

One of the early lessons I learned from Professor Higgins was the value of anger and frustration as agents for change. Determined to show no fear—another legacy from my Marine dad—I relied on what I knew. Success starts by setting goals. Catapulted by anger and frustration, I began to imagine goals I could set for my son.

Goal setting helped to calm me. I clearly recall the day I sat in my living room chair, looked at my beautiful baby and uttered a huge sigh of relief as I pulled myself out of the quicksand of doubt and fear to a familiar ground of believing we could achieve anything we worked hard enough for. And I was aiming high enough for Christopher to be seen and have my idea of a happy future.

A few weeks later I began to research again, this time seeking only positive information about capabilities, statistics or anything about potential possibilities for children with Trisomy 21. I couldn't find any non-clinical reference materials in our local library. Why not? Reports studying institutionalized people reported only what people with Down syndrome couldn't do—they didn't address what they *could do.*

It wasn't right! My frustration inspired me and gave me a purpose. What if I could help Chris show the world what he *could* do?

I didn't know where to begin, but having a purpose gave me hope. And that was a good place to start. I felt stronger with the resolve to help my son make a difference in the world—even with his unique diagnosis. Finding nothing concrete to justify my belief that Chris could attain my lofty goals didn't stop me.

Simply pretending to believe in possibilities for my son helped me to lean into our unknown future. Holding tightly to the teachings of my parents about goals and work ethic firmly grounded me.

Loaded with good intentions, I embarked on my journey to mold and sculpt my son as his mother, personal tutor, trainer, and motivator. With me at his side, my baby boy would one day break through limiting ideas and outdated expectations. I vowed that Christopher would be one of the first men with Down syndrome to excel enough to be an influencer in the world. I envisioned him making national news as the first boy with Down syndrome to achieve the rank of Eagle Scout with the Boy Scouts of

America. He could be successful in sports with the right coaching. He might contribute in some way to the educational and scientific communities, and even speak to the United States Congress. These goals focused my energy away from fear of the unknown and toward an earnest curiosity of what could happen. (But I didn't tell anyone about my secret goals—especially family members—because I didn't want to deal with any more pity or pessimism.)

I immersed myself not only in all the current information I could find on Trisomy 21, but also in learning how to tutor my child. Knowledge is power, and the ultimate power I wanted to offer my son would be to successfully teach, push, pull, and inspire him to learn and develop. I committed myself to being dedicated enough to do whatever he needed, even if it meant controlling everything in Christopher's life.

Eventually, through the next few lessons I refer to as "Undergraduate Courses," Professor Higgins showed me how knowledge is different from wisdom. He taught me that rather than being in control, I needed to value and learn how "to be."

My real education began when I started to let go. Unchaining Christopher from my goals and domination opened space in my mind to receive what the universe was offering to teach me (and the world) through him.

Before learning the power of "letting go," I thought my son's life without notable success would be a life without purpose or meaning. I hadn't realized my son had one of the greatest purposes of all—he was born to teach.

LESSON 4
Trisomy 21: There's Much More Up Than Down

It was 1979, a few months after Christopher's first birthday. I was nine months pregnant and attending an evening Lamaze class with my husband. A Nurse Practitioner began the class that evening with a discussion on potential birth abnormalities. I felt a heavy sense of fear in the room from the other expectant parents. My compassion for them turned to shock, however, when the instructor responded to one woman's question about healthy eating by saying, "Don't worry too much, it's not like you're going to give birth to a Mongoloid freak..."

I gasped and jerked straight up in my seat, inflamed and combat ready to respond to her offensive insult. Using the archaic, racist term *Mongoloid* combined with *freak* created a whirlpool in my stomach which drained all hope that people outside my circle of family and friends would accept my son. I once read about that horrible old term but knew the scientific and medical community no longer considered its use appropriate. I couldn't believe a Nurse Practitioner could be so ignorant and callous to say it publicly.

Hot blood pulsed through my entire body and my heart pounded with anger. I earnestly wanted not only to correct the teacher, but also say something that could ameliorate the heavy feelings of dread in the room. I felt compelled to explain how my son's so-called "abnormalities" were a gift to us, and that we experienced happiness and love as any other parents do—perhaps more.

Sensing the intensity of my emotions, my husband gently placed his hand on my leg. He leaned in close and whispered, "Don't say anything yet. Just give it a minute."

He was right. I drew in several slow deep breaths to bridle my rage and focused on choosing words I could say to educate the instructor without alienating her. A few minutes later when a break was announced, my husband and I approached the teacher who was surrounded by several parents asking her questions. Eventually, we introduced ourselves and explained our first child's diagnosis of Down syndrome.

"I'm so sorry," she said.

I took another deep breath to keep my outrage suppressed and carefully explained, "Well, that's just it. We're not sorry. It's definitely not as bad as you inferred by the words *freak* and *Mongoloid*. I wonder if you know the term 'Mongoloid' is no longer used because it more accurately refers to a nationality—to the people of

Mongolia—and comes across as a slur? And our son is *not* a freak. He's actually really cute and…"

I'm not sure she heard anything I said, because she interrupted me with some hasty and flimsy explanation of why she used the term and then abruptly turned her back to us and began speaking to another couple. My husband and I were dumbfounded at her rudeness in brushing us off. Clearly, she wasn't interested in hearing our perspective. We looked at each other in disbelief and turned to walk back to our seats.

"I didn't know your son has Down syndrome." I turned in the direction of the woman's voice and saw a friend I had talked with in previous classes.

"Oh hi! Yes, he's one year old now." I smiled.

"What's it like?" she asked.

The genuine sincerity in her voice felt respectful and we welcomed her question. My husband and I eagerly shared how charming our son was, described his sweet disposition, and the increase of love in our home.

She hesitated but continued, "Are you worried about your son's impact on your new baby? What the dynamics might be?"

"Umm…" I couldn't think of a satisfactory answer. "All kids have an impact on their siblings." My mouth was speaking, but my mind was frozen by her question.

She continued, "Then, you don't worry about how much time your son may need, and if that will take your attention away from your next child?"

My mouth opened to speak, but no words came. The realization that we'd never thought about it hit me hard. To us, our son was simply like any other baby. Was I a thoughtless, shallow mother to not have fairly considered whether our other children would be impacted by Christopher's medical diagnosis?

"No, we're not that worried." I tried to sound confident but inside I was shaken. My husband pulled at my arm, stating he needed to get a drink before the class restarted. I thanked my friend for her frank questions, and we beelined toward the drinking fountain at the back of the room.

"Thanks for saving me. I just wasn't ready for those conversations." I sighed when we were out of earshot of the others. I looked at him with defeat in my eyes.

"Let's just leave," He whispered, and I readily agreed.

We never returned to our seats or to that class.

Alone together in the car, my emotions overflowed. I vented my anger over the haughty, ignorant instructor, frustration about my inability to sway her from her obtuse opinion, and self-doubts over my pathetic responses to my friend's questions. My husband agreed and admitted to feeling the same way. We had to face the harsh reality that our son may never be fully accepted in the world and some people might treat him like a freak.

My pain at these thoughts was so intense I could no longer speak. We sat in silence for the remainder of the drive home. My husband handled his anger stoically and never fully explained his thoughts to me. I cried and felt very alone. I recall wondering why he didn't cry or show signs of sadness although I knew he was equally downcast. His inability to share his emotions just increased my sorrow for our family.

Later that night when I couldn't sleep, I began to consider what it might be like to have a brother with a severe mental impairment. I tried to envision the impact through a child's perspective. I wasn't even sure yet what negative impact there would be. We hadn't yet experienced any adverse effects of our son's diagnosis—except for the negative reactions of other people. The challenge to understand our unknown future was too difficult, leaving me lost and depressed.

Why hadn't I worried about any repercussions on a future child before getting pregnant? Was I setting up my son and our new baby for unfair hardships? Was I self-centered? I was mad at myself for being so naïve or slow to see beyond my own joy in our son. Self-deprecating introspection only made my depression worse. Eventually I decided that without real answers, all I could do was be curious about our family's future. One day at I time, we'll discover whatever the effects are.

Kathryn was born a few weeks later and Tara arrived as a surprise the following year. By the time Chris turned four in 1982, I had filed for divorce. Ultimately, having three children in three years was too overwhelming for my ex-husband and he moved across the country to be near his parents.

Being a single mom without much support meant Kathryn and Tara (and I) needed to become as self-sufficient as possible as soon as possible. To their credit, my young girls grew up quickly and without complaint about how much I relied on them.

The day Kathryn started crawling before Chris, she became my oldest child. As she grew, she became her brother's biggest cheerleader, role model and protector. When I was away at work or school, she was his interpreter and translated his mumblings and sign language to their caregivers.

Speaking for Chris began when she could barely speak herself, and she continued to be his advocate into adulthood. She encouraged his love of singing, acting and being a jokester. Kathryn was not only a gift to me and her little sister, but a godsend to Chris as well. She helped me value the imaginative playful side of Chris. Not only did Kath really understand Chris—to his core—but she always got his back. Just like a second mother, she was nurturing and thoughtful about his needs. Kathryn was so strong, loving and caring that there may have been several years—especially while I was attending college—when he might not have known which of us was the real mother of the family.

Tara also took on a nurturing role and went out of her way to include Chris—to entertain him and make sure he never felt left out. When she was in junior high school, I typed a homework assignment she handwrote about her experience having a brother with Down syndrome. I was blown away when she called her brother "a huge gift." She said, "His heart is so big it overflows into the hearts of everyone in the family." Referring to herself as his "big little sister," she explained that she "never had to *learn* how to have compassion and kindness for others." Her brother instilled in her "a strong desire to protect those who couldn't protect themselves or didn't have a voice."

I've often noticed with pride how Tara seemed naturally compassionate toward others and made new friends easily. "This trait," she explained "developed because of Chris. I was constantly on the lookout for those who had less in life and tried to include them. I noticed kids who sat alone during lunch at school and invited them to sit with me and my friends." To this day, Tara continues to befriend and help many, and she attributes her capacity to care about others as "a gift Chris gave me which I am determined to my children."

During her high school years, Tara included her brother in her friend group, and they adopted him as an equal. This group was pivotal in Chris' life because he was seen and treated as merely another teenager. They teased each other, quoted movie lines and didn't seem to mind when Chris used our only TV to watch the same movies over and over. They talked about their various love interests and laughed when Chris flagrantly flirted with all the girls. They just hung out and ate everything they could find in my pantry. On the days I arrived home from work and found my son with Tara and her friends there, my heart soared. I didn't even object when my grocery bills tripled. Thanks to Tara, Chris had friends. And perhaps thanks to Chris, Tara had exceptionally good-hearted friends.

After I married Brian, a kind and gentle man who accepted my three children with open arms, our daughter Aubrey was born in 1989. Chris was eleven years old and readily welcomed Brian as his father. Aubrey is the only child in the family who Chris considers a younger sibling—even though he is the oldest. He has protected her since she was a baby. For example, one afternoon, after I placed Aubrey in her highchair for lunch, Tara and Kathryn came into the kitchen to ask me for something. The conversation became heated. (I don't recall exactly why—it could've been because they wanted to go somewhere, and I had other plans.) But it wasn't long before Chris walked into the middle of the room and pointed his finger at my face.

"Be nice!" he commanded. "Baby sad." Everyone looked at little Aubrey who was sitting quietly and staring wide-eyed at us. We realized our argument negatively impacted everyone in the family, not just us. We fell silent. I was immediately sorry for overwhelming Aubrey as well as humbled by Chris' sensitivity to her feelings. Without being in the room, he had been aware of emotions in Aubrey which I had overlooked.

As she grew, Aubrey revealed a loving and compassionate nature. On one occasion, when complimenting her empathy for others, she replied, "Chris had a lot to do with that."

"How?" I asked.

"I think," she continued, "it was because Chris was non-verbal, and I had to learn early in my life to use different ways to communicate with him. I figured out how to recognize and read his physical cues, facial expressions, familiar mumblings and even his hand gestures to understand him or have a conversation."

I was struck by her wisdom as she explained, "When I grew older, I wanted a deeper relationship with him. Since I knew he struggled to explain his thoughts I decided to first figure out what was important to him so I could fully understand him and what he says."

Aubrey became so in tune with Chris' feelings that she often felt them herself, even without Chris saying anything. For example, one evening when Chris was in his late 20's, Aubrey and I were having dinner with him in a restaurant. Chris wasn't saying much — as usual. Aubrey and I were absorbed in an intense conversation about our worry for the welfare of a struggling family member.

While focusing intently on Aubrey, I was surprised when she abruptly interrupted me by turning to Chris and asking him what was wrong. She reached over and placed her hand gently on his arm and began to stroke it.

She turned to me and said, "He's really sad."

Chris didn't answer, but slowly shook his head "no." I was bewildered by Aubrey's reaction but noticed that Chris was slouched over with his chin almost on the table.

I quietly asked, "What's going on Buddy? Are you sad?" Chris remained silent but looked up at us.

Aubrey said, "I think something's terribly wrong. Then we both saw it—a single tear fell from his eye and rolled down his cheek.

We both lunged to hug him and begged him to explain.

After a minute he said, "They made fun a me." He jerked his head in the direction of the table next to us. "Called me *netarded*."

We both gasped and feverishly talked on top of each other. "They couldn't be talking about you!" I exclaimed. Someone at the next table must have said the "R-word" loud enough for Chris to hear, but I was too engrossed with our conversation and didn't hear it.

"They have no idea what that word means!" Aubrey hugged him tighter. "They're using the wrong word and don't know that it means something beautiful."

We held Chris, poured love over him, and reassured him until we could cheer him up with some dessert. Chocolate did the trick.

"How did you know something was wrong?" I later asked Aubrey.

"Out of the corner of my eye, I saw his head hanging low. As I looked at him, a wave of sadness poured over my body, and I knew it was coming from him."

"Wow! I'm so grateful for your empathy—what a gift to us."

The daily practice of tuning into her brother's needs helped Aubrey become more caring and empathic not only to him, but also to others. She has explained, that "having Chris as her brother changed her thought patterns and leveled up her consciousness."

When Chris was eighteen, sadly Brian and I divorced. It was an amicable decision and not based on any difficult issues pertaining to Chris—in fact, he still calls Brian his dad. But being a single parent again meant that Chris' siblings regularly cared for him, particularly after school.

Six years later, my sister and best friend, Becky, died. She was only 41 years old with children still in their teenage years. I later adopted her sons, Jared and Jason and my family expanded again. It just felt right because I always loved them as my own. I was the proud mother of three girls and three boys; Chris was especially happy to finally have brothers. To this day he randomly calls them just to serenade them. "We are brothers, and we will fight for you," he shouts with fervor the words to one of his favorite songs from *The Newsies*.

Jared, who is five months younger than Chris, is our family's board game enthusiast. He goes out of his way to include Chris in family games and credits Chris for teaching him a higher level of patience and unconditional love. Jared takes everyone else to task if we don't strictly follow the rules, but never seems to mind when Chris doesn't. When called out or corrected by another one of his siblings, Chris responds with a wink and a smile or a shimmy and a *"hee-hee."* And Jared gets his back. This *"hee-hee"* has become our family's tagline whenever there is a wild twist or turn in any game. Eventually it has been extended to lighten our mood when any unexpected event or embarrassing moment occurs. Our family laughs and enjoys the dynamics of games—and life in general—more intensely with Chris' "anything goes" attitude.

Jared explained to me how Chris taught him about unconditional love. "When experiencing my darkest days and at times when I didn't feel like I was enough, Chris always greeted me enthusiastically with a smile and a side hug. Even though I never shared my hardships with him, I always felt loved and accepted for being myself—his brother. He taught me about the power of acceptance without limitations or expectations."

Jason, our family's kind, gentle peacemaker, is three years younger than Chris. He values Chris' loving nature and wholeheartedly agrees that Chis is the superglue in our family. When sharing what he admires most about Chris Jason said, "no matter what emotional situation we're each going through, he is always there with open arms."

Jason once explained that during big family gatherings when the conversation became intense or turned to politics, he sometimes mentally checked out. He wondered if somehow Chris could tell because "Chris often makes his way over to me, sits down, smiles or flexes his arm and asks me to feel his muscles. He's the brother who can really see through me sometimes and shows his love with playfulness."

At last, I can answer the question posed by that sweet, worried woman in my Lamaze class so many years ago. I'm pleased to report that a family member with Down syndrome has an uplifting and life altering effect on siblings, parents, cousins and everyone who is willing to see him with their hearts. Actually, it's one of the upsides which we weren't expecting. (*Hee-Hee!*)

As a mother, some of the foremost dreams I had for my children were for them to learn empathy, compassion and acceptance of others. Because of Professor Higgins' influence, I never needed to teach these lessons. And there is no way I could've coached my children in a more profound and impactful manner. Our family was gifted with *the* finest teacher in Professor Higgins. I'm grateful I didn't hesitate to bring so many siblings into our family.

Naivete can be a good thing.

UNDERGRADUATE COURSES

LESSON 5

An Unintended Education:
Wake Up and Smell the Chocolate

I don't know where I acquired my false belief that children are supposed to be a lot like their parents, but it wasn't long before I began to notice Chris' unique personality unfold through his unconventional preferences and behaviors. We could not have been more *dissimilar*. But it was OK, I was ready to teach him how to become like me.

Chris was an easy baby. Quite the opposite of my high strung personality, Chris was zen. He just looked around and watched, rarely crying—unless he was hungry. Not surprisingly, eating has remained one of his top priorities (and greatest joys) throughout his life. Other than food, he seemed to have no personal agenda (or goals). He was a "go with the flow" baby and readily molded his needs and wants into my daily routines. Those were the days I thought mothering was going to be super easy.

By the time Chris was six months old however, I realized I needed to start pushing a little harder for him to achieve "normal" milestones. He was well past the typical age of rolling over or making baby sounds, but he just peacefully and quietly enjoyed the view from his baby carrier. When I discovered that some babies his age were even beginning to crawl, it was "go time" for me to increase my efforts to become his dedicated tutor and show some results.

I attended a National Symposium on Down syndrome and found experts to connect with as advisors. This, and similar conferences helped me meet other like-minded parents who were hopeful and optimistically committed to changing the outlook and future possibilities for our children. These resources boosted my enthusiasm to work more with my son.

I became doggedly determined to help Chris learn and to help him catch up as I noticed other milestones not being accomplished. For example, he didn't hold anything—a spoon or even his bottle. I didn't know if he didn't care or whether his muscle tone was too relaxed. So, we added little hand muscle strengthening workouts to the therapy we were attending three times a week. During these sessions I carefully watched the therapists pattern him in rolling over, standing, sitting, and essentially every type of movement he might need one day. I copiously took notes and asked a lot of questions in order to use the same techniques with him at home. I purchased similar toys and therapy tools for our daily practice but wasn't seeing significant results. Chris was simply fine watching me or looking around the room, while sitting in his baby carrier, on my lap or while lying on a blanket.

Nothing motivated him to move. Chris showed no interest.

Although months passed and Chris was still not rolling over, I wasn't deterred. Was I worried? Yes, but not enough to taper down or give up on my goals for him. Since Chris suffered with constant colds through the winter months, I blamed his lack of progress on his health, not on my inability to motivate or teach him. Fighting off a cold took 100% of his little body's concentration and energy. When I discovered his milk allergy and converted him to soy formula, a sparkle returned to his eyes, he stopped getting sick, and he was more alert. But he remained unable (or disinterested) in doing any major movements on his own. He simply enjoyed being held and cuddled.

Finally, we had a breakthrough when Chris was about ten months old. However, I don't deserve any credit for it.

It was the night before Easter Sunday when I placed Chris on a blanket in the center of our living room while my sister and I scattered colorful Easter Eggs and candy for her four year old daughter to find the next morning. Because he had yet to roll over without assistance, I knew the baby and candy were safe enough for us to leave the room.

Five minutes later I returned to find Chris six feet

away from his blanket with candy stuffed in his mouth and fists.

I gasped. "How did he get there? He had never moved anywhere before!"

I yelled for my sister to see what Chris had done while I removed as much candy as I could from his mouth. I returned Chris to his blanket and stepped back to see if we could crack the code on how he got across the room. Within seconds he rolled back to the candy, a scenario he repeated over and over. I was elated he had learned to move so far and so quickly in only a few minutes!

Before that evening, the only milestones Chris had accomplished were eating and smiling. And although he was incredibly talented at both, he never grasped a bottle or spoon as tightly as he held onto that Easter candy! Although we hadn't seen any improvement throughout his months of therapy, apparently Chris *had been learning* how to use his fingers and roll over—he just hadn't seen the need for it.

Chocolate became my secret weapon to motivate Chris to move. He soon mastered rolling around so adeptly and quickly rolling that his classic move was nicknamed his Tootsie Roll.

I looked forward to showing off Chris' skill to his therapists, but at our next session when I proudly held out my hand with an M&M and called Chris to come to me, they were neither impressed nor amused. They refused to endorse giving such a young child candy—and of course they were right. Without bribery, however, Chris wouldn't roll in their presence for weeks. Finally, one day he did—but it was on his terms and in his time frame.

Armed with a new insight into what motivated Chris, I was excited for his next milestone of learning to crawl. But nope. He may have occasionally moved a knee on his own, but he zoomed around rooms so well with his Tootsie Roll that he wasn't interested in crawling. His bottom line was that rolling took less effort to get where he wanted to go. His sister, Kathryn, who was fifteen months younger crawled before he did. (It was a piece of cake to train her, but no, I did not use chocolate!) It was months later before he officially crawled, and even longer to walk—in his unique way—with an M&M buried tightly in each little fist.

Chris' ability to move around was an easy challenge compared to teaching him to speak—to use words. In his defense, his tongue was too large for his mouth. For years he was unwilling to even try to articulate. All words sounded like the same "Humh," or similar guttural noises. It was a miserable season of guessing what Chris wanted when I couldn't understand him. I desperately needed Chris to communicate.

I didn't give up easily on my desire to coach Chris and control his progress in all aspects of his life. At this point my life was unraveling. I had filed for divorce, I needed to get a job and wouldn't be able to spend so much time helping Chris. All my three children were under the age of four, but because of Chris' slow development, I felt as if I had a three year old (Kathryn) and twin two year olds (Tara and Chris). Soon both of his younger sisters surpassed Chris' developmental level. I recall holding daily preschool lessons and papering the family room walls with the alphabet train and other reading tools. I was in constant tutoring mode.

I was weary, yes. But, giving up was not an option. Throughout the divorce, my need to control all the chaotic aspects of my life—and Christopher's—was even stronger. I worked obsessively with his mobility, speech, reading and writing. I refused to give up on my dream for Chris to be able to speak publicly and be an example of success. The more topsy-turvy my life became, the tighter I held on to Chris and his sisters.

One day, I discovered Chris mimicking basic sign language and we all quickly got on board and learned American Sign Language (ASL). Chris understood what we were saying, but it was challenging to figure out many of Chris' signs. His chunky little fingers and his haphazard movements looked more like improvised gestures. I used to joke that he even mumbled in sign language. No matter how his signs looked to others, they were beautiful to me because finally he could communicate! We gratefully and successfully relied on sign language for many years.

When Chris was about six, he woke me up early one morning by patting my hand and saying, "Locky Mow." I had never heard those words before and had no idea what he wanted.

I peeked at him through barely opened eyes and saw him standing next to my bed leaning his head near mine. In a husky morning voice I replied, "I don't know those words, use all your words, Buddy," I had worked until 2:00 a.m. the night before and was desperate for more sleep. But I was proud of myself for remembering to use the phrases the speech therapists taught me instead of just ordering him to "speak clearly."

"Locky Mow." Chris repeated, and repeated and repeated, until I finally rolled out of bed with a loud groan.

With my eyes glued shut, I fumbled to place my finger in Chris' little hand and cleared my throat. "Show me what you want, Buddy."

Chris walked me to the kitchen, sat down in the middle of the room, looked up and asked in a hopeful tone, "Locky Mow?"

"I don't know those words. Show me what you want." I repeated and peeked through the tiny slits my eyes had become.

Chris didn't budge. He looked up at me with pleading eyes and begged, "Locky Mow?"

"Do you want a cookie?" I made the sign for cookie — cupping my right hand over my left. (In my defense, I was sleep deprived and desperate to return to bed.)

He didn't nod or shake his head. "Locky Mow." He whined.

"Cracker?" I guessed. I tapped my right fist on my left elbow. He usually loved Graham Crackers.

"Lockyyy Mowww." His whines turned to moans and he began to rock back and forth in misery. For what seemed like 30 minutes, I opened every cupboard in the kitchen and named everything I could see. Once his moans turned to wails, I would've given him anything— even ice cream—to appease him so I could abate both of our misery and return to bed. Someone else could watch Chris for the hour of extra sleep I so badly needed.

Discouraged and depressed, I gave up and sat on the floor next to Chris who was now hunched into a ball. He was whimpering "Lockyy Moww," so pathetically I started crying along with him. Completely out of ideas, I instinctively resorted to saying a prayer.

"God, please translate for my son. I need help." I said out loud without really expecting an answer.

"Chocolate milk?" As I heard the words come out of my mouth, I doubted the instantaneous translation. Chris jerked his head up and looked at me with a huge grin.

"LOCKY MOW!" He yelled jubilantly. He threw his body into my lap and hugged me, delighted to have been understood.

My tears of frustration turned to tears of gratitude. Forgive my lack of faith but as I sat on my kitchen floor hugging my young son, my entire soul was awake and electrified with joy. What a shock that my prayer had been answered so quickly and so distinctly. The translation clearly hadn't been my idea! I would've never guessed he was saying, "chocolate milk." And the Instant Breakfast™ was right there—in the pantry, but I had somehow skipped past it.

That was the unforgettable day I learned through my Professor Higgins how God cares about the tears and desires of little children—no matter how seemingly insignificant—as well as a mother's sincere desire to help her son. Also, I learned that results can be better than expected, when I am open to the unusual.

Sitting down at the table watching him enjoy his glass of cold chocolate milk (sans cookies), I pondered how my controlled plan for Chris' developmental progress hadn't turned out as I'd intended. Instead, things had been better! My slow-to-walk and slow-to-talk son had been a successful teacher. Perhaps he's the only one who could have taught me how to let go and believe that things can work out well on their own. If Chris hadn't learned things in his own unique way and timing, I wouldn't have been entertained for so long when he was little by his Tootsie Roll, and I might never have learned to translate Chris' thoughts without words.

It was time for me to wake up and smell the choco-late—to let go of being overly invested in achieving pre-conceived outcomes—and learn that all I need is "to be." Just "being" meant that I need only do my best from one minute to the next. When letting go of my desired results, the real education came with the understanding that it's all good enough.

To this day, my kids and even some of my grandkids call chocolate milk "Locky Mow." Whenever I hear it, I grin and am grateful to be able to understand Chris by his glance, grunt or smile, and am reminded of the potential for better results when I am open to the unexpected.

LESSON 6

Tapping Out:
Finding Happiness In Acceptance

I didn't sign Chris up for Peewee Sports when he was young because he couldn't keep up with the other boys his age. I waited for him to get a little older and hoped he would one day choose to participate in a mainstream sport such as basketball or soccer. Meanwhile, when Chris was only seven years old in the mid-1980's, he discovered wrestling entertainment on TV. It was love at first sight for Chris.

I was appalled the first time I heard the clangor of men yelling threats and the thud of them hitting each other or the mat. Upon hearing the pandemonium, I bolted into the family room.

"What's all the ruckus about?" I demanded. To my chagrin, cute little Chris bounced on his knees and pointed to the TV shouting, "Eee-Hee!" His sweet face looked as giddy as when spotting Santa at Christmastime. It was not only my first introduction to World Wrestling

Federation (WWF), but also the beginning of a long nightmare for me.

"That's disgusting." I changed the TV channel. There was no way I was allowing this trashy influence in my home.

"No! No! No!" Chris wailed. He threw himself on the floor and yelled unintelligible sounds over and over. Eventually, I deciphered the name "Hulk Hogan" who would become Chris' first All-American Hero.

Whenever he could, Chris would sneak into the family room and click through the channels until he found his beloved "Royal Rumble." My tenacity in changing the channel was equaled and outdone by Chris' consistency in changing the channel back the moment I left the room. Until I could afford a second TV, battles raged both in our family and on our television.

I've never evolved past my original appalled reaction to what I deem neanderthal entertainment. How could I consider an activity where men in tights slam each other with chairs and tables, a real sport? And the impropriety of women in skimpy bikinis throwing each other around a fighting ring speaks for itself. I couldn't fathom the attraction to mindless body slamming, yet the more violent and crass the fight, the more Chris' blue-grey eyes sparkled with enjoyment.

As he grew older Chris continued to be an undeterred wrestling fanatic. I admit, I was excruciatingly embarrassed about his passion and continually tried to redirect him, but Chris couldn't run (or wouldn't) and wanted nothing to do with team sports.

Although I reserved the right to act like a martyr, I eventually gave in and let him watch WWF because of Chris's loyalty and the intensity of his happiness. Nothing else could match the excitement WWF brought to him. My otherwise non-verbal, mellow son cheered his favorite wrestlers and booed their opponents. For the first time he initiated long, incoherent conversations about the backstories of many of the fictional characters. The conversations were difficult to endure because his speech was hard to understand, but I squelched my desire to constantly remind Chris that "they're not real" and encouraged his talking.

Over the years, his infatuation became worse. In his nightly prayers, he passionately prayed for wrestlers who died or had been injured. Whenever we traveled or met people from a particular city, he rambled off names of wrestlers from their hometown. It was unfolding before my eyes how amateur wrestling had become a lifeline for Chris to connect to the outside world.

I never thought I would be grateful for Chris' speech difficulties, but when we were socializing, I was relieved when others couldn't understand his babble about The Undertaker, The Ultimate Warrior or Hollywood Hulk Hogan.

Against my elitist standards, I conceded and allowed Chris to watch WWF as long as he kept the volume low.

But when I left the room, the boisterous, booming sounds of the combat vibrated against my spine. My capitulation to this tasteless entertainment became a guilty secret. Although I feared being judged a negligent mother, I comforted myself in knowing Chris had no propensity for violence and watching wrestling wouldn't change him. Still, when the doorbell rang if WWF was on TV, I quickly turned off the mayhem to protect my secret indiscretion.

Originally, our family only had to live through *Monday Night Nitro*, but Chris wasn't WWF's only fan. Eventually, wrestling monopolized two and later, three nights of our week. Excursions to the video rental store to select a family movie turned into a struggle as Chris begged to rent some type of *Smackdown*™. I invariably agreed, but only after scanning the store to make sure nobody would recognize us.

As Chris grew older his obsession intensified exponentially. My hope of him growing out of his addiction crashed in 2002 when WWF became World Wrestling Entertainment™ (WWE). He remained a dedicated fan, collecting wrestling figures and asking for WWE Magazines for Christmas and birthdays. He studied the pictures for hours, ripped out his favorites and taped them to his bedroom walls.

Chris and I had a never-ending argument about whether his beloved wrestling could be considered a legitimate sport. I usually shook my head and said, "This is fake. These guys are *not* real wrestlers, they're actors."

Chris would jut his chin out and growl, "wesling is weal!"

Neither of us budged. We remained rivals in our own battle royale.

I resented WWE taking over our family evening hours. Friday nights became a ritual streaming of *Friday Night Nitro*. Because I couldn't leave Chris alone, Friday nights were miserable. When we were out, he would start pulling on my sleeve at dusk to remind me we needed to go home. He couldn't tell the time but figured out that the sun setting meant WWE would be on TV soon. Either our family was unhappy being stuck home on a Friday night, or Chris was miserable when we were out.

"Don't worry Buddy, we'll be home before the time wrestling starts," I assured him over and over. But Chris didn't trust me to get him home on time. I tried to avoid his gaze—which was more like a glare—but when he caught my eye, he clenched his teeth and pointed to his watch-less wrist reminding me to check the time. Chris was completely and annoyingly dedicated to entertainment wrestling.

Years later, the fateful day came when I was forced out of the closet—the night the bishop, who was the leader of our local church congregation, came over for dinner. I thought it was cute when twelve year old Chris offered to say the blessing for the food, but he had an ulterior motive. He sabotaged my secret. Although he mumbled through a few sentences such as, "thankfulforthefood" and "pleaseblessit..." he surprised us all by saying, as clear as day, "Please bless mom to know...westling...is...weal. Hulk Hogan is good. He is a...a...a...hewo."

My head jerked up while Chris was still praying, and I glared at him. He was staring directly at me. With a smug "gotcha" look on his face he said, "Amen."

I got busy passing bowls of food while my face heated in a fierce blush.

"So, Chris, you like wrestling?" the bishop broke the awkward silence.

"Uh huh!" Chris had a distinct twinkle in his eyes as he bounced up and down.

My heart sank a bit. My slim hope that the bishop couldn't decipher Chris's speech was dashed. I knew him to be a kind man who regularly went out of his way to talk with Chris at church and respectfully include him in classroom discussions. They had a warm friendship.

"Tell us about your favorite wrestlers." The bishop's smile felt respectful; it seemed that he genuinely cared about those bizarrely clad mercenaries.

"Have some potatoes," I urged the bishop. But the wrestling aficionados were not to be deterred. The conversation went on...and on. Chris talked about several of his favorite wrestlers, and I was stunned when the bishop also named a few. I had to resist covering my face with my hands to cool the hot blood burning my cheeks.

If I couldn't beat 'em, I guess I had to join 'em. My

girls couldn't conceal their giggles as I pretended to be supportive of Chris' wrestling fetish. But inside, I was dying of embarrassment. Once again, I had been reminded not to underestimate Chris' abilities. In his perspective, he had gone over my head—to both God and the ward bishop—to override my resistance to WWE.

Having our family's dark secret exposed had an unexpected impact on me. Watching Chris and our bishop have a genuine discussion over something I had judged as bad gave me cause to pause. My son had made a real connection in the world through his love for amateur wrestling. And the bishop's acceptance of Chris, shown by his respectful, kind interest in engaging Chris in such a lengthy discussion, somehow liberated me.

I had concealed my embarrassment over Chris' amateur wrestling fetish long enough. The bishop's cheerful and calm acceptance of Chris shifted me to finally support my twelve-year-old son's passion. Perhaps this was a goal he wanted to achieve. I found a gym offering private wrestling lessons. Based on the owner's assurance they could provide necessary accommodations, I signed Chris up.

When I shared the good news with Chris that he would be going to a wrestling class, I laughed as he erupted into a happy dance. Chris' sisters appeared equally delighted that his wrestling fantasies could become reality and insisted on going with him to his first class. (I assured them all, of course, that there would not be any brutal assaults with chairs or chains, but that it would be a more finessed type of wrestling.)

When we pulled into the parking lot of the gym, Chris began jumping up and down in the back seat. We were early, so once inside we waited at the side of the floor mats for the class in progress to end. Chris' eyes opened wide as he focused intently on the wrestling dual in front of us. Finally, it was Chris' turn and the coach called Chris onto the mat.

Chris jerked his head to look at me with wide eyes. I nodded my encouragement and smiled.

Chris shook his head "no" in rapid fire and backed up against the wall with the back of his hands in front of his face. "No, no, no, no…" Chris insisted. He plopped down on the floor and sat cross-legged. I tried to pull him up with his arm to get him to stand, but his legs remained tightly crossed. Despite my coaxing, Chris refused to budge. The coach took me aside to talk about possible strategies to engage Chris while his sisters continued to encourage him.

Out of the corner of my eye I saw Chris suddenly jump up and dart towards the front door yelling, "TOO DANGEROUS!" He burst through the metal gym door and ran into the parking lot. My daughters and I were dumbfounded and stared at each other. We'd never seen Chris run like that before.

The awareness of Chris being alone in the parking lot jolted me from my astonished stupor. "Oh, my gosh I gotta go!" I yelled to the coach as I ran outside with my daughters right beside me. We found Chris with his fingers clenched around the door handle of our locked car. He refused to relax his grip until I assured him we were going home, and he didn't have to stay in the wrestling class.

Apparently, Chris' favorite sport is being an armchair wrestler—all passion, no participation.

Chris' enthusiasm for WWE has only increased over the years. It remains at the core of his happiness and reason for living. And WWE continues to be emblematic of everything I stand against. During those early years when we both refused to "tap out," the tension between us was occasionally far worse than the pandemonium in the ring.

When Chris was young, my secretive and insincere support of Chris' fetish only caused my humiliation to grow—blocking both my ability to change and his connection with the world. Following that liberating dinner when our bishop bonded with Chris over wrestling, I thought deeply about why I had been so concerned about others' judgments of me.

By never "tapping out" on his commitment to WWE, my Professor Higgins taught me how acceptance is freeing. Our bishop's endorsement of Chris' love for WWE without a whit of judgment softened my heart. I was able to look at why the opinions of others about the respectability of entertainment wrestling and my parenting had weighed so heavily on me. I eventually realized that it wasn't other people's judgments I was worrying about—they were my own. It wasn't the need for respect from others that had burdened me for so long—I had been trying to prove to myself that I was a good mother, even though deep down I considered myself negligent for allowing my son to watch such class-less violence. And my personal bias was blocking Chris off from possible connections in the world.

But why would I be so judgmental or even care about something as ridiculous as entertainment wrestling? This question required a deep dive into my inner self which unfolded memories of my mother, and my grandmother. Eventually, I sensed generational elitism and a strong desire to be highly regarded by others. That discovery astonished me because I detested pretentiousness—almost as much as I despised WWE. And then it hit me. Was I a snob? Ouch! (This is where acceptance can get a little painful.)

With this new awareness, I needed to choose between my need to be right and Chris' happiness—which meant that I had to choose to embrace my hoity-toity biases or entertainment wrestling. Easy decision—Chris's happiness wins. I tapped out and surrendered.

That was the moment I willingly dropped my objections and accepted entertainment wrestling as my son's favorite sport. This unexpected lesson was my first introduction to the liberating concept of "surrendering." I define it as the willingness to embrace and accept reality without bias or unfair judgment. I learned that surrendering entails more than resignation. I needed to understand that "it is what it is." My acceptance meant I was more committed to my son's happiness than to make him do things my way. My focus shifted from when Chris would change, to accepting what makes him most happy.

Philosophically, I remain an advocate for improvement. There are many problems in the world worthy of change. But, knowing when to encourage change in others or whether change is needed in me has been one of my most complex and essential lessons to learn. My wish for the world would be for everyone to discover something to be as passionate about in life as Professor Higgins has found in WWE.

My early goal for Chris to participate in mainstream sports was well-intentioned to help him find something he's good at and can feel good about. He never showed any desire to engage in activities in which he would break a sweat. He was, however, actively engaged in simply being content and excited. If happiness were a work-out, even if achieved sitting in a chair, Chris would be one buff dude!

LESSON 7

Joy In Surrendering:
Who the [Bleep] is Dennis?

O ver the years my parents, uncles and aunts occasionally expressed their admiration to me for the
way I raised Chris. They praised how I helped him "fit
into a normal life," or, the way our family "just seemed
normal." However, their attempts to compliment the way
I parent my child with Down syndrome never landed well
with me. Unsure how to reply, I politely thanked them
with a feigned smile and simply changed the subject.

Their comments left me feeling empty and I wondered what they meant. What was normal? Was it a
genuine standard for success? In truth, there was no
normalcy about my family. In many respects, our way of
life was far better than normal, and I was puzzled why my
extended family members couldn't readily see it. Their
words of praise seeded a desire in me to raise children,
including Chris, to be anything but normal.

When he was younger, I constantly looked for ways to

help Chris raise the low expectations which doctors, some therapists, teachers and all of society seemed to have for him. But after reflection over his first ten years of life, it seemed clear I was the one being transformed. My attitude had shifted about the possibilities for my son and accepting him on his terms.

One day when Chris was about ten years old, we ran across an old friend of mine whom I hadn't seen since high school. After exchanging pleasant greetings, I put my arm around Chris and proudly introduced him. "This is my oldest child, Chris."

"Dennis." Chris promptly and boldly corrected me as he confidently extended his arm for a handshake. My friend's face looked quizzical as she gingerly shook his hand. I was momentarily flabbergasted by Chris' announcement and amused by my friend's surprised reaction but rolled with it.

"Oh, excuse me," I said with a faked grimace. "I meant Dennis. Apparently, although he's ten, we're still up in the air about his name." I laughed at my own joke because I enjoyed the times when Chris would surprise me. (And truth is, the situation was funny!)

My friend didn't laugh. Her frozen smile loomed uncomfortably large. "Hmm," was her only reply. I wasn't sure whether she was unnerved by the confusion over his name or by noticing my son's Down syndrome features.

I was surprised by Chris' new name but embraced the entertainment. "Life is never dull in our family!" I chuckled and changed the subject.

During dinner that night I invited Chris to share his big news with the family.

"Chris has an announcement for everyone."

"Hmh?" Chris asked.

"Tell them your new name, Buddy."

"Dennis." He didn't miss a beat as he casually reached for another roll.

Chris nodded as I told the story of meeting my old friend and offered no explanation why he decided to have a new name. Everyone shared a hearty laugh when I described the perplexed look on my friend's face. No one was surprised; we had become accustomed to Chris' unconventional ways and welcomed a new entertaining episode. (Who's lucky enough to have a family this fun?)

"You want Dennis to be your nickname?" Tara asked. "Nope." Chris shook his head.

"You want a completely new name?" He nodded at my question.

"Dennis, it is!" Tara patted Chris on the back. "Way to go after what you want, Buddy."

Since Chris had watched the movie *Dennis The Menace* maybe a hundred times, we all immediately knew why he picked his new name. Initially, we thought his taking on the persona of this cheeky character was cute.

Until it was *not*.

Chris' attachment to his new name wasn't just a passing fancy. He remained committed to it—far too long.

During the "Dennis years," he ignored us when we didn't refer to him as Dennis and wouldn't come when called. Other times he corrected us when we didn't use his new name. Every, "please bless Chris..." in family prayers triggered his bold whisper, "Dennis!"

His consistent corrections became a bit annoying at times—especially in public. Close friends went along with us on Chris' new identity, but others had no idea how to react. The entire family was astounded the day I stood at the pulpit in church giving a talk and referred to my son by his name, "Chris." He immediately stood up from his seat with the family in the audience. I hesitantly continued speaking but cringed as I watched him leave the aisle and walk to my side.

"Hello, Chris. Welcome," I said. "I'm sort of in the middle of something here. Do you want to say something?"

He leaned in closely to the microphone. "I am Dennis."

"Oh, I keep forgetting his name." I highlighted my sarcasm with an eye roll and exaggerated grimace. I wasn't that concerned; we were amongst friends and almost everyone in the audience was smiling. I pointed him to the empty seat next to the bishop and nudged him toward it. The bishop caught my cue and kept his arm around Chris for the remainder of my talk. After church, several friends approached us asking Chris about his new name and we all enjoyed a hearty laugh together.

The Dennis years rolled on. While part of me was secretly proud of Chris' focus and long term dedication to anything, choosing his own new name became like a symbolic billboard showing me what little influence I truly had over his likes and dislikes. This was a tough pill for me to swallow, but ultimately—quite the potent medicine.

There was a bright side to the Dennis persona. I was pleased when I noticed that the more Chris acted out his impish alter ego of *Dennis the Menace*, the more confident he became in his sense of humor. He enjoyed being a rascal, which eventually morphed into becoming a prankster as well.

One of his favorite tricks was slipping random superfluous items into my shopping cart in stores. Usually, I'd find them before checking out. But when he surreptitiously began to help me by putting our purchases on the checkout counter, I didn't discover them until we arrived home.

"Hee! Hee! Hee!" He chuckled when we got home, and he pulled out his cache of treasures from our bags. He'd waive a fuzzy toy, pop tarts, or a whoopie cushion at me. It was cute the first few times, but the added burden of saving receipts and making returns wore me down. (I let him keep the woopie cushions—his favorite comedic prop.) On more than one occasion, a visitor to our home *accidentally* sat on one. Other times Chris (oh, I meant Dennis) jumped out from hiding to startle our guests. We quickly learned that hearing Chris' sniggering was a clue to be careful before sitting down. His sisters were especially on alert when their friends were over.

Before the Dennis years, I had already passed through enough years of transformative experiences to learn the importance of being flexible, embracing the unexpected, letting go of judgment and finding joy in riding the wave with my son. This ability to surrender now opened doors for Chris to connect to others in a new, unique way. We felt lucky because at that time it was just the comedic relief our family needed.

Although much of Chris' identity as Dennis was charming, I couldn't fully give up on his real name. But he was committed and continued to correct me whenever I didn't call him by his new name, or he purposefully ignored me.

Then one dreadful day, all entertainment from Chris' fantasy identity exploded when I lost him in a store at the mall. He was almost twelve years old. After a few frantic minutes of darting through the aisles yelling for Chris, I begged a clerk for help. I tried to stay calm and collected when describing what he was wearing but broke down as I explained his inability to speak clearly, and because he had Down syndrome he appeared and acted much younger. The clerk was sympathetic and responded immediately by summoning Mall Security and enrolling another clerk to watch the door as she helped me search the store again. The longer we looked, the more terrified I became that my vulnerable child had been kidnapped. Deep fear constricted my ability to breathe, and I struggled to think clearly. I was consumed with thoughts of what a kidnapper might do upon discovering Chris' diagnosis.

My head was spinning, and I was weak. His disappearance could be fatal.

The Mall Security Officer finally arrived and asked me to retrace my steps with him to the spot where I last saw my son. After writing down Chris' identifying information, he pulled out his radio. Hearing him broadcast my son's description somehow snapped my mind back to reality. As soon as I heard him say, "the child's name is Chris Higgins," it clicked.

"Dennis!" I yelled. "No, wait officer! He goes by the name of Dennis!"

The officer eyed me curiously.

Immediately, Chris popped out from behind a line of clothes hanging against the wall and swaggered toward me, triumphant over his successful prank.

"Hee! Hee! Hee!" He flaunted a mischievous grin. Nobody else was amused.

I gasped with relief, fell to my knees and hugged Chris. I didn't know whether to squeeze him tighter or yell at him. But I couldn't speak through my tears. Out of the corner of my eye I saw the quizzical looks on the faces of the store clerks and security officer who must have wondered why I didn't know my own son's name. Perhaps they questioned whether I was a kidnapper? I didn't try to explain myself—I barely had the strength to talk. After proffering my sincere thanks and apologies in halting speech, I left the store tightly grasping Chris's hand.

"Buddy, your name is *not* Dennis!" I scolded Chris as soon as I felt calm enough to speak. Once we reached the parking lot, I knelt next to him before getting into the car. I looked him squarely in the eyes and said, "You can *never* hide from me in stores! It will *never* be funny! I was so scared I'd lost you—for forever." I started to cry again.

He frowned, touched my face with his small hand and wiped away my tears.

He got it.

A short time later and without explanation, he started to use the name Chris again. Dennis had enjoyed a good run, but I was happy for the season of the Dennis years to end.

I pondered why Chris' decision to become Dennis was so tough for me to fully give into. Other than being embarrassed by how eccentric it was, his fanciful decision wasn't that big of a deal. Since Chris' birth, nothing had gone as I'd planned—at least not the way I'd expected. And now, he wouldn't even give me the basic parental prerogative of choosing his name.

The ability to surrender was continuing to be a difficult concept for me to master—courtesy of my military father who constantly taught me to never give up or give in (except on issues he wanted to control *in my life*). That was it! I didn't want to give up control over what was clearly a parent's prerogative—choosing a child's name. I wondered if I needed to learn this lesson at an entirely new level.

My young son's choice to assume a different name symbolized his desire to make life choices independent of what I wanted. My annoyance shifted to joy and laughter as I saw Chris revel in the liberty of picking his own name. I noticed how the freedom I gave him facilitated more self-confidence and an opportunity for him to blossom into a jokester. Choosing to be someone who makes our world a happier place was unexpected, but a better outcome than any of the goals I had previously set for him.

It took having a great teacher like Professor Higgins to teach me that I didn't always have to win or be in control of situations. Refusing to surrender can be appropriate for war but not for everyday life—and especially not for fostering loving, supportive relationships. I needed to learn that surrendering did not always mean failure.

I would've never guessed I'd one day be thankful that Chris was my first child. But for the unparalleled teachings of Professor Higgins, I'm not sure I could've learned the value of surrendering as well from my other children. I could've easily been annoyed by Chris's stubborn fantasy that he could magically become a television character. Instead, with the lessons I learned about acceptance and letting go, I willingly stepped through the looking glass to enjoy the view from Chris' perspective.

Thanks to his unique way of teaching me, Professor Higgins showed me ways to let go of my expectations and need for control over my children, so our family wouldn't turn out to be too "normal." Allowing my children the opportunity to create their own individual personas brought many surprising experiences. It made me realize how grateful I was that my family was *not* normal.

What is a "normal" family anyway? I am happy to have escaped from the prior generational thinking that everyone needed to fit in or appear successful according to obscure and ever-changing societal norms. What would have been the price we would've had to pay for being conventional?

Instead of looking at my children and imagining who I can mold them to become, I choose to be open to the possibilities of how they will mold me. Stepping into being my best self allows me to be a better influence on them as I continually offer them advice and direction. This can be the reward of surrendering to my children's right to have some autonomy in their lives.

The Dennis years transformed the entire family. We each did our part to help eradicate "normal." Chris discovered his love of being a jokester and making others laugh with his shenanigans, and we learned the value of giving him the space to be himself.

To this day, Chris has never met a whoopie cushion he doesn't like. If you come to our home and hear quiet snickering, you'd better look around before sitting down or be ready to join in on the fun.

LESSON 8

Expectations And Badges: The Merit Of Letting Go

E ven before I was married, I was certain my future sons would achieve an Eagle Scout award from the Boy Scouts of America. It was a family tradition mothers expected of their sons. My own mother proudly wore the Mother's Pin given to her when my brother earned his Eagle Scout and prominently displayed it in her jewelry box.

We celebrated Chris' fourteenth birthday with a trip to the Army/Navy store to buy his uniform and, of course, his first pocketknife. We hyped up his involvement with Scouts and Chris seemed happy to join in. My husband, Brian, was a new Scoutmaster and was proudly ready to give Chris any extra assistance to help him adapt to the rigors of camping, hiking and other adventures. We were both happy to help him earn merit badges and looked forward to seeing how his scouting experience would enrich his life with fun adventures and great achievements.

Before his first Scout meeting, I sewed the numbers and patches on his freshly tailored uniform. We *oohed* and *aahed* as he posed before the mirror. I envisioned him one day wearing badges which would eventually be framed and hung on his bedroom wall for the rest of his life to showcase his accomplishments. I happily envisioned the future day when I would be presented the Eagle Scout Mother's Pin, with everyone cheering my son—the first boy with Down syndrome to earn the prestigious award. In my mind, my son would be one step closer to showing the world his abilities and value. Chris smiled at his handsome reflection and danced a little jig. He had no idea what was ahead for him.

Neither did I.

The summer of Chris' first year, the Scout team planned a weeklong camping trip hiking in the San Gorgonio Mountains in southern California. As we usually did when easing him into new things, we talked with him often and described the upcoming trip in detail. He didn't say much during our dinner conversations which turned into family motivational pep talks.

"Chris, camping in the mountains is going to be so much fun! You're going to love it!" I beamed with pride.

"Eee-hee." Chris focused on his food.

"Boy Scouts are cool, Buddy. You'll have fun!" his twelve year old sister, Tara, chimed in. Chris took a bite of food and grunted.

"Are you excited for our fun hike?" Brian asked.

"Uhm." Chris wasn't excited. But he seemed happy enough and he trusted us.

On Saturday, three days before the Scout trip, our son sat on the floor of the garage and watched us fill his pack. His father placed many items in his own pack to keep Chris's pack as light as possible. We coaxed him to stand as Brian placed the backpack straps around Chris's arms while continuing to lift most of its weight. But when Brian let go and Chris felt the pack's full weight, he went limp and pulled his arms free from the pack which crashed on the floor next to his collapsed body.

"Toooheavy!" Chris moaned.

Brian didn't give up. He graciously emptied Chris' pack of more items and added them to his own bulging pack. Brian and I shared a worried look. I looked through our camping supplies for a lighter pack. My secret fear that Chris was physically unable to backpack seemed to be materializing. Chris had extremely low energy and weak muscle tone. He could walk but even at theme parks, he needed encouragement to keep going all day. I'd never seen Chris endure truly strenuous activities. But Brian assured me again that after the initial hike to their main campsite, their trip would be more about swimming and outdoor fun. I brushed off my fears and assumed with sufficient motivation Chris could enjoy the camping adventure with his dad and the other boys.

Early on the morning of their camping trip, I made

pancakes to start Chris off happy and to ensure he was willing to leave with his dad. Even with all our encouragement, deep down I worried he wasn't fully on board—and didn't understand what camping would be like. As my guys walked out the door, I handed them a bag of treats with a side of lunch, and waved goodbye so enthusiastically my arm ached. I breathed a long sigh of contentment as they drove off, confident my dreams for Chris' happiness were coming true.

Five days later, Chris stumbled through the front door with Brian close behind. They were so dirty and disheveled I barely recognized them. I hooted with laughter, but my grin froze when Chris staggered toward me wearing a deep frown. He threw himself into my arms and hugged me so tightly I couldn't ignore his distress. The fake grin on Brian's face confirmed my fear. Something had gone terribly wrong.

"Are you OK?" I leaned back and pried Chris's arms off. He pointed to the corner of his eye. I knew the move—I'd seen it many times. He wanted me to know he was crying, even though I couldn't see any tears.

"Everything turned out fine." Brian's attempt to assure me bombed.

"What's wrong, Buddy?" I asked. "Didn't you have a fun time with all the boys?" He buried his face deeper into my shoulder and held on tighter.

"What happened? Is everything OK?" I shot Brian a questioning look.

Brian shook his head "no," but said, "We had fun, didn't we Bud?"

Chris didn't move and didn't speak.

"Chris never gave up!" Brian added in an upbeat tone. "He lasted the whole time."

"No. More. Boy. Scouts." Chris mumbled woefully into my shoulder.

I patted Chris' head and back for a few moments before pulling him away and gently ushered him upstairs, into a hot shower. As soon as I could leave Chris alone, I found Brian unpacking his truck in the garage and again asked what happened. Brian sat down on the tailgate and began to share the traumatic details of their scout trip.

"Chris did OK for about the first 300 yards after we left the truck." Brian said. "With constant encouragement he walked about 15 minutes, but the trail became much steeper than anyone expected, and it was too hard for him. At one point he just sat down and refused to go further."

"Oh, no!" I braced for more bad news. "How steep was the hike?"

"Well, apparently, I misunderstood the distance between the contour lines on the black and white copy of the topographic map we used to plan the trip. A color version of the map might've been more helpful to show the actual terrain." He grimaced.

Brian slowly explained, "the symbols on the topo map which I thought were campsites were actually mountain peaks. Rookie mistake—I'm embarrassed to admit it and I feel so bad."

My eyes opened wide.

He coughed back a nervous laugh and continued, "It was a super steep hike and not appropriate for young, inexperienced hikers. Especially not for Chris."

I winced but didn't interrupt.

"Luckily, there were a lot of fathers with us. The only way we could get Chris to move was for one of us to carry his pack—while one boy took his hand to pull him up the trail another pushed him."

"Oh no!" I exhaled a long moan.

"When pushing and pulling no longer worked, most took turns carrying Chris on their shoulders or backs. He walked only a short distance the entire hike—mainly on the flat or downhill parts of the trail."

"Poor Buddy!" I sighed and placed my forehead in the palm of my hand. "Poor everyone! How did the other boys handle it? Were they upset?" I cringed. "Was anyone mean to Chris?"

"The hike was hard on each of us, but much too difficult for Chris. I should've brought him home early and almost did. I wanted to. We talked about it on the trail and at the campfire the first night, but everyone encouraged me to stay and offered to help Chris, even if it meant carrying him and an extra backpack...Brian's voice broke. You wouldn't believe how generous and kind everyone was." He wiped away a tear.

I was touched by Brian's tenderness and sat speechless—almost breathless—waiting for him to continue.

"A few times two boys linked their arms to make a chair for Chris and some even suggested making a stretcher out of fallen trees and tents to pull him."

I blinked back tears as my husband explained how everyone cared for Chris without any complaints. He shared what the other fathers and leaders said in admiration of the boys' strength, endurance, and willingness to sacrifice. His voice quivered as he relayed how everybody on the trip encouraged Chris to stay, because they wanted him to reach the meadow and the lake where he would have fun fishing and swimming.

"It was amazing to see how the boys and leaders bonded through hard-core service," he said. "Everyone in the troop came together to get Chris through the ordeal and while doing so, they all bonded and became good friends."

Kathryn and Tara arrived home later in the afternoon, missing all the drama. During dinner Tara asked, "So, how was your Boy Scout trip, Buddy?"

"No more Boy Scouts," Chris grumbled without looking up from his food. Kathryn stroked his arm and looked at me questioningly. I knew his sisters were worried, but I shook my head and motioned to kill the conversation.

After dinner, Chris snuggled next to me on the couch to watch a movie. He didn't speak another word until I tucked him into bed that night. He looked at me with pathetic eyes and whimpered, "No more Boy Scouts?"

"No Boy Scouts tonight, My Buddy." I tucked his sheets closely around him and stroked his hair.

"You did an incredibly hard thing My Buddy. I'm proud of you. You were strong. Who helped you?"

Chris didn't answer.

"Your dad helped you. He will always be there for you. Your friends helped you. You are one lucky duck to have good friends! And your family will make sure you'll always have someone to help you. Don't worry. If you don't want to go on a hike like that one ever again, you won't have to."

"No Boy Scouts." Chris whispered and nestled into his cozy bed with a big smile, glad to be back in his room in his comfortable life.

Following his mountain climb ordeal, everything about Boy Scouts was tainted for Chris. He never again put on his Boy Scout uniform. Sad over the wasted time and money, I suggested framing his uniform to hang on his bedroom wall. He growled and said, "No. No Boy Scouts."

As long as his father was Scoutmaster, we encouraged Chris to go to scout meetings and activities. He went reluctantly, but mainly to see his friends who carried him up and down those steep mountains. These friendships continued through the rest of his school years.

It wasn't long before we stopped pushing Chris to attend scouts. Initially, I was disappointed recalling how — before his one and only hike — he seemed so proud of himself in uniform as he looked in the mirror. But perhaps it was my pride—my gushing over him—he had smiled about, not his own future dreams or expectations. I had been so intent on doing what I thought was best for him that I failed to find out if Chris ever wanted to participate in Scouts. He had simply gone along with my ideas trusting me, as always.

My ultimate goal was for Chris to be happy. I thought being successful as an Eagle Scout—and all the adventures building up to receiving that award—would make him happy. But truth is, Chris becoming an Eagle Scout was about making *me* happy. I donated his scout uniform.

"No Boy Scouts?" Over the thirty years since his one big scouting adventure, Chris has asked me this question hundreds of times when I'm tucking him in at night. It's become our secret code for me to remind him that he is safe. Each time Chris nestled happily under his covers with my assurance of "no Boy Scouts," my heart smiled. And each time I am reminded how complete joy feels— knowing my child felt safe, loved and content in our family and home. Chris never needed external evidence of accomplishments, such as a badge or title to be happy. And neither should I.

This was how Professor Higgins taught me the importance of being willing to let go of my nonessential expectations for my children, and the importance of accepting their preferences. This is a classic example of how hard it can be to navigate parenting—to know when to stretch our children to try to accomplish more, and to know when to support their choices. There is no easy answer.

In giving up my dream of framed merit badges and an Eagle Scout Mother's Pin, I also relinquished the misguided belief that my goal should be his. It wasn't easy to surrender a dream I'd had for Chris since he was a baby—that I would help him become successful and make a notable impact in the world. Chris didn't care about any of that but ultimately, he did make a big difference in the world—in his own way—for all who let him into their lives.

Although he never earned a single merit badge or passed any ranks, Chris was successful in Scouting because he made good friends. Those boys and their dads who served Chris so magnanimously remained welcoming and kind to him for many years following that grueling hike. Perhaps the Boy Scouts of America should give merit badges for making true friends. Certainly, there should be a badge for anyone who carries someone up or down a mountain!

I was changed by Chris' involvement in Scouts but not in the same way others usually are. I discovered that the only Mother's Award I really want is one Professor Higgins could pin on me for being a parent who lets her children choose their own dreams.

MASTER'S COURSES

LESSON 9

The Chris Game—
Learning To Enjoy The Ride

Our family road trips have always included singing because of Chris' enthusiastic love for music and his fervent desire to entertain us with his musical gifts. In Chris' (apparently) tone-deaf world, his musical performances are worthy of stardom. He is confident in his belief of one day being discovered as an off-the-charts Hollywood rockstar. And I agree with half of his dream— that he's off. His talent is clearly off any charts; he dances and sings off-beat, off-key, off-pitch, off-tune, off-lyrics, off-harmony and even off-octave.

There is no courteous way to describe Chris' musical abilities other than to say he has the singing talent only a mother could love.

But, oh how Chris loves to sing! Our road trips morphed from carpool karaoke to road concert tours. He sings, no matter who is in the car, or who can hear him when we're at a stop light. To him—the more fans the better. He acts as if he sincerely thinks his entertainment is a favor. Chris doesn't only belt out his favorite rock 'n' roll oldies, musicals and Disney™ tunes, he performs. Although his short legs dangle a few inches above the floorboard and the seatbelt inhibits most of his movement, he performs like a master of air dancing during his cover of Elvis' *Blue Suede Shoes* and *Jail House Rock*. And he's a virtuoso of the air guitar when performing *Johnny B. Goode* by Chuck Berry.

From their earliest years his siblings and cousins joined right in and had a blast. Chris usually grabbed the coveted front passenger seat to play the air piano on the dashboard for some performances, such as *Great Balls of Fire!* by Jerry Lee Lewis. As lead vocalist he was backed up with air drums and other air instruments feverously played by the others from the back seat. We kept the music loud during those jam sessions and everyone sang at the top of their lungs.

We rarely traveled by air before my children grew up and moved out, but Chris was miserable when we did. I wouldn't let him listen to music on a headset because it was impossible for him to resist singing along. This made road concert tours in our car our favorite option.

His siblings and cousins were cool. Whenever they grew tired of the never-ending concert, they would put on noise cancelling headsets and let their brother do his thing. Losing his band members never bothered Chris — he continued with solo performances for the remainder of our drives. Evvvvvery minute, no matter how long the trip or what time of night, Chris regaled us with choreographed musicals. The only breaks he took were during pit stops or when he was eating—why I always packed plenty of snacks.

For years, our family traveling band happily performed, until things changed when his youngest sister became old enough to voice her opinions. Aubrey is eleven years younger than Chris. When she was about five, she wasn't quite accepting of the long concerts—especially after an hour or two into each trip. And nobody really blamed her.

"Mom, can we *please* turn off the music? Chris' singing is driving me crazy," Aubrey normally pleaded after she could no longer endure singing along or wearing a noise cancelling headset.

"Come on dear, be patient. Your brother is happy when he's singing! Please let him enjoy himself?" I usually begged right back.

"It's not fairrrr!" Aubrey's whines eventually turned to wails when she was little. "You always give in to him!"

"He thinks he's entertaining *us* and helping to make *us* as happy as he is." I tried to explain Chris' perspective, but my efforts yielded only a futile repeat of the same argument every time. She was too young to understand.

Aubrey either kindly suffered in silence or cried. Eventually Aubrey's cries triggered Chris to sing louder in an attempt to console her. Thus, the cycle became increasingly difficult to endure.

I also unsuccessfully tried to get Chris to compromise. I explained that Aubrey wasn't dissing his singing, but she was bored or needed to sleep. She also wanted to play games or talk with her sisters. But our requests only seemed to offend him. He couldn't understand why his talent wasn't enough to keep everyone happy.

For what seemed like forever, neither Aubrey nor Chris would compromise. I felt as if I was trying to negotiate with two five-year-olds. The situation presented a quintessential parental conundrum for any family— which child should be favored?

Aubrey was correct that I usually gave in to Chris. Before she was born, our family revolved around Chris' needs, without issue. But this travel problem was the first scenario when both Chris at age sixteen, and Aubrey at five, were intellectually similar and at an impasse. Should I cut the proverbial baby in half and require each child to compromise equally, continue to indulge my son, or cut off his endless concerts?

At first, I tried forcing a compromise. Either Chris was singing and Aubrey was crying, or Aubrey was peaceful, and Chris was miserable. When I intervened with forced intermissions of his performances, Chris brooded and shed a few of his own tears. And so it went, mile after mile, hour after hour. Thus, our longer car travels usually ended with one, both and even me in tears.

I never gave up trying different strategies to resolve our

dilemma. There had to be a solution other than waiting for Aubrey to mature and accept her brother's rockstar fantasy. On occasion, I gave Chris a headset but we didn't find the peace I'd hoped for. It's hard to say which torture was harder to bear—singing along with Chris for six to twelve hours with the music blaring, or him using a headset and enduring his loud, tuneless word salad without the benefit of music.

It was this furnace of misery and desperation which forged an idea for a new road trip game. We named it *The Chris Game*.

"I have a fun idea!" fifteen year old Tara announced during one eight hour road trip. She reached over and lifted the headset from Aubrey's ears.

"Want to play a game with us?"

Aubrey removed the headphones. "Yes, anything! I'm soooo bored."

"We're all going to guess what song Chris is singing." Tara put Aubrey's headphones on Chris and set up his music to randomly select songs out of order, making it difficult to know which song he would sing. We agreed to some rules, such as awarding one point to the first person to correctly guess each song, with five points winning the game and a special treat at the next pit stop.

We were surprised how challenging the game turned out to be. Without being able to hear the music or lyrics, we struggled to identify the song. Each song's words were either mumbled, abbreviated, or slurred past with a long, meandering note. The harder we struggled to shout out the name of the song, the heartier we laughed! Chris was encouraged by our enjoyment and became increasingly animated in his performances.

We played *The Chris Game* for years until we eventually had all his versions of our family favorites memorized and Aubrey finally grew old enough to patiently enjoy Chris' touring concerts along with her older sisters and cousins. Our family still enjoys happy memories of *The Chris Game* which carried us through Aubrey's younger years.

His siblings no longer travel with us by car. These days I'm the entire audience and his only band member, but he's still the lead vocalist. At the end of every song if I forget to give him a "thumbs up" or compliment his performance, he asks me if I like it. Of course, I do.

When I can't take the discordant sounds any longer, I have found myself singing off tune on purpose. When slurring words and singing random sounds along with Chris, I've been surprised to find peace within the chaotic concert. On occasion I noticed how zen-like such a concert could be. It was almost therapeutic inside the clamor as I released any desire for control. Could this be what heavy metal fans experience?

This delightful lesson on finding happiness even in cacophonic chaos taught me that surrendering doesn't always look like simply giving in or giving up. More than accepting situations or others as they are, surrendering can be fun and invoke peace.

For our family it helped us to embrace both Chris and Aubrey's perspectives and find creative ways to enjoy the ride together.

As I pondered the lessons Professor Higgins offered me (with his Assistant Professor—Tara), I realized how letting go of control can be a key to finding peace. Our family jam sessions symbolically reflect how I accommodate Chris in my life. He may appear discordant to others, but when stepping inside his unique musical sounds with a sense of playfulness we have found joy and peace.

LESSON 10

Chris Presley—
Living His Dreams In His Own Key

Elvis Presley's music has had a particularly enchanting influence on little Chris. Whenever he heard it, he leapt up to dance, even before he had the physical coordination to run or jump. Long before Chris could walk or talk clearly, he could rock 'n' roll.

Chris' love of dancing is surpassed only by his passion for singing. As described earlier, he sings boldly and loudly with confidence that everyone within earshot enjoys his musical talent. Truth is, we do, but it has been an acquired taste.

I encouraged his love of music in the privacy of our home or car but was hesitant to let anyone outside of the family hear or see Chris perform. Fearing that those who didn't love him wouldn't be as accepting as our family was, I wanted to protect Chris from any possible ridicule.

However, when Chris was about 10 and his sisters started taking piano and singing lessons, he also asked for singing lessons.

"I be Mr. Hollywood...Elvis Presley." He said with a toothy and jagged grin. "Sing too?"

"I'm not sure their teacher has openings, Buddy." I lied.

Chris' grin turned quickly to an exaggerated frown that speared my heart.

"But I can ask!" I smiled. Chris turned and bounced with happiness as he walked away.

I was torn. I never wanted to be the one to tread on Chris dreams, but I didn't think any teacher would agree to lessons after hearing Chris sing, and I worried he would be crushed by the denial. But I didn't have the heart to be the crusher.

I stalled Chris for a few weeks, but one afternoon Chris decided he could no longer wait. As soon as Kathryn's lesson ended, he walked to the piano and faced their teacher, Jeanie Hawks.

"Iam...Mr. Hollywood. I sing?" He mumbled in his low, monotone voice.

"What?" Jeanie looked at me to translate.

"Well...um...Chris is hoping to one day take singing lessons like his sisters." I explained nervously.

"Oh, that's nice. You like to sing?" She asked Chris.

"Eeee-Hee." He replied and pointed to the piano. I knew that was his cue for her to play a song to show her his singing talent. (After all, he didn't need much warm-up for his skill level.)

"What songs does he know?" Jeanie seemed forced but willing to go along momentarily.

"Oh, any Disney or Elvis song." I grinned nervously. "You can pretty well play anything, and he'll sing along."

Chris nodded, bursting with excitement. He almost seemed to grow two inches as he belted out a one minute version of *When You Wish Upon a Star*.

Jeanie giggled and thanked him. Otherwise, she was speechless and looked at me to break the silence. I congratulated Chris and asked his sisters to take him outside to wait for me. They were great at distracting him.

As soon as they left, I explained Chris' dream to be a singer, how tone deaf he (obviously) was, and how it takes an earful of love to enjoy his music. After I asked if she would consider adding a half hour lesson for him each week. She smiled but apologized as she said that she didn't feel qualified to work with Chris. I added that I'd attend every lesson to help translate for him and explained my willingness to pay for lessons only because they would make him happy. I emphasized how wonderful it would be for him to have the same opportunities as his sisters and assured her I had no serious expectation of improvement in Chris' musical abilities.

"I guess we could try. Let's just have one lesson and see what we can do," she offered hesitantly.

I thanked her and left after arranging the time. His sisters and I cheered when I shared the good news of his upcoming lesson but said it may only be one and sort of like an audition. He didn't hear my warning and burst into a little shimmy, kicking one foot up with joy. His belief of one day being a famous singer like Elvis carried him happily forward.

When I arrived home after work on the day of his first lesson, I found Chris sitting by the front door holding a large bag. I smiled when I saw his blue suede shoes and slicked-back hair plastered with gel. He had apparently packed his bag with a tape recorder and several of his favorite Elvis tapes for accompaniment. I had assumed that he would just sing a song Jeanie selected from a Broadway musical. (He knew them all!) But he apparently had planned exactly how he wanted his performance to turn out. He was ready!

During his sisters' lessons Chris' knees shook with anticipation while he not-so-patiently waited for his turn. He was holding the tape recorder he had taken from its bag and carefully picked one tape to place inside. I whispered in his ear, "Don't be nervous. Jeanie's gonna love you."

"I ready." He whispered back with a slow, purposeful wink.

When Jeanie finally called his name, Chris jumped up, took his place next to the piano, nodded his head at Jeanie and hit play on his recorder. I don't think I was breathing as I watched him. He sang his heart out, kicked his feet and even threw in a few spins. Chris' confidence and enthusiasm won Jeanie over in seconds. She burst out in giggles and started to play along with the taped music. At the end of their exhilarating mini concert, she beamed, "after that, how could I say no?" My face was sore from smiling so broadly. I finally exhaled.

"Eee-Hee!" Chris held both arms out to receive applause and nodded, as if to say, "Of course! I'm a natural!"

When Jeanie asked what types of songs they could work on together, I assured her he had an infinite repertoire. He could sing any song if someone else is also singing. And I explained that he doesn't rely on lyrics but has an impressive ability of imitating words with the slightest delay.

"But don't worry," I added with a grin. "The delay is rarely noticeable because it is so overshadowed by his pitch, as you probably already noticed." Jeanie never stopped smiling until we said goodbye. Chris had successfully enrolled both of us in his dream, and we were his loyal groupies. I was only sorry that I hadn't thought to sign him up earlier!

Chris danced all the way to the car. His eyes sparked with happiness as we all congratulated him on passing his audition so successfully!

Chris' weekly singing lessons were so much fun. His teacher, sisters and I couldn't wipe the smiles off our faces as he sang—off tune and slightly delayed—especially when he added impromptu dance moves. During those thirty minute lessons, Chris became a musical celebrity. Jeanie later told me Chris' lesson was her favorite each week because the time spent with him "shifted her mood and filled her home with joy." I nodded my understanding and expressed my delight at being able to share my son's superpowers with her.

Not long after starting lessons Chris began asking, "YoucallHollywood?"

"They're super busy, Buddy. But they'll probably find you—they're always looking for extraordinary talent." I lied.

After a few months of lessons, Jeanie surprised me with the suggestion of Chris singing at his upcoming baptism in church. I voiced my concern that it would be a disaster for him to sing in public because he is so off tune. I could foresee guests squirming in their seats trying to endure his singing and told her of my deep fear of Chris being publicly mocked. I didn't think my heart could handle seeing anyone laugh at him and was determined to protect him from ever being treated as weird or an outcast. Truth was, one day I'd eventually admit that I had been protecting myself more than him.

"Although it may sound like Chris is off tune to us," Jeanie assured me, "he consistently sings on pitch. I've noticed he sings in a key which is exactly two octaves plus a flat lower than the original key of the song." She added that she had been experimenting with her theory during singing lessons and thought she could adjust her accompaniment for any song using this musical algorithm.

It became an easy decision to let Chris sing as part of

his baptism program because only friends and family were invited. Jeanie and I spent the next few weeks helping him learn the words to his solo. The morning of his baptism, he bounded out of bed and put on his new suit hours before the scheduled time. (I had previously won the argument about whether sequins could be added to the suit. I'm proud to say I held the line—no sequins!)

He marched into the baptistry that afternoon with his head high, looking debonair in his new blue suit, white shirt and white pocket square folded smartly and tucked in his handkerchief pocket. I noticed him looking around for someone.

"Who are you looking for Buddy?" I whispered.

"Hollywood."

"Buddy, today is your day. You're getting baptized. All these people are here because they love you. It's not a Hollywood sort of day." I feigned seriousness, but inside I smiled. No doubt the opportunity to sing for a real audience vastly overshadowed any excitement about his baptism.

Chris sang *I Am a Child of God* with passion and fervor—two octaves plus a flat lower. There wasn't a dry eye in the house—a palpable spirit of love and unconditional acceptance filled the room. I glanced at Jeanie through my own watery eyes, grateful for her support of Chris's dreams. I could tell that she was struggling to see the music and play the piano while wiping away tears. Chris' enthusiasm for singing reminded everyone in the audience of the value of every person—including those with unique tones.

Ever since his successful debut, Chris has held onto his dream to entertain audiences as a singer. He continued music lessons and although they didn't improve his ability to sing on pitch or in tune, they did improve his confidence and articulation. I noted that the singing lessons improved his speech articulation much more than his years of speech therapy.

In the afternoons, after returning home from school (or years later, when he returned home from Care-Rite, his work/day program), he enjoyed singing with his karaoke machine in his bedroom—of course with his widow opened wide to serenade the neighborhood. There were many days when I returned home from work, and upon opening my car door in the driveway my mood immediately brightened just hearing Chris' tunes through his bedroom window. On sweltering summer evenings, I would shake my head and sigh when I saw Chris's window wide open, worrying about my air conditioning bill. Chris shook off my lectures about wasting money, as if it was simply the cost of stardom. Luckily, our kind neighbors never lodged noise complaints with city officials or me. (Although I tried to preemptively win them over by introducing myself and Chris to new neighbors with gifts of fruit and an explanation for any singing they might hear—which might sound more like a hound dog.)

"I am Elvis." Chris offered as his excuse.

On Chris' twenty-first birthday our family celebrated with a trip to Las Vegas to fulfill his lifelong dream to see Elvis live. (I didn't have the heart to tell him "live" did not mean he's still "alive.") At the time a talented artist named Steve Connolly performed SPIRIT OF THE KING on the backlot of the MGM Grand Hotel. Chris packed his suitcase days before we left and polished his performance of every Elvis song in his collection in anticipation of his dream birthday trip.

We arrived at the show early because the seats weren't assigned—they were on a first come, first choice basis. We found great front row seats close to the stairs to the stage, (which were cordoned off with ropes) and next to the speakers. I hoped the loud music would drown out Chris' singing, if I couldn't contain his exuberance.

Once the King of Rock appeared, Chris couldn't stay seated. Everyone in the family exchanged huge grins as we watched his hip-swinging dancing. But when the song 'Blue Suede Shoes' started, Chris couldn't contain his excitement any longer. He darted away. I lunged for him but didn't grab him fast enough. He ran up the stairs and out to the middle of the stage and immediately broke into dance—about ten feet from Elvis. I chased him but stopped at the edge of the stage. My screams to Chris were drowned out by the music and cheers of the crowd. My hands flew to cover my mouth as I held my breath, worried Elvis would stop the show in frustration, or whether Chris might be roughed up or yanked off the stage by security.

I panicked and ran to a Security Officer screaming, "I'm his mother!"

The Security Officer shouted "Look!" He pointed at Elvis who had his hand raised at security to stop them from approaching Chris. Elvis continued his performance without skipping a beat while Chris danced a few feet away, copying Elvis' every gyration. Elvis ended in his classic pose with a mic in one hand and his other arm held high. Chris copied the same pose with his attention proudly fixed on his idol. The crowd cheered wildly.

"Ladies and Gentlemen," Elvis walked the few steps to Chris and put his arm around him, "My little brotha!" The crowd's roar melted both my heart and my deepest fear. Chris bowed to the crowd, then turned and bowed to Elvis before strutting off the stage with a final jubilant wave to the audience, as if he was the star they were cheering.

Tears poured down my face. I could barely see to grab Chris' hand to walk him back to our seats. We enjoyed the rest of the show from our seats (with a corner of Chris' shirt held tightly in my hand). Elvis also kept an eye on Chris and occasionally even gave him his famous "pointy finger" acknowledgment.

After the show, many kind audience members waved to Chris or gave him a thumbs up and yelled, "great job brother of Elvis!" We waited to see Steve Connolly who patted Chris on the back with a "hey brotha! You were great out there!"

Chris beamed—he was flying high from fulfilling his life-long dream. I could barely speak to thank Steve for his graciousness to our son. Although I was embarrassed of my free-flowing tears, I sputtered a few words to explain my gratitude for the powerful, transformative impact his generosity had on Chris and on me. I'm sure Steve could see my sincerity through my stammering and tear-filled eyes. Before that time, I had only shared my worst fear for Chris to his singing teacher—that he would be publicly mocked or shamed. I was overflowing with happiness and gratitude for everyone's acceptance of my son.

Clearly it was inappropriate for Chris to run onto the stage. Everyone could have reacted with the same shock and horror I was feeling, but with Elvis' cue, the audience accepted Chris and even cheered him. Their unfettered genuine applause for Chris proved my longstanding fears had been unfounded. And Chris' vision of dancing and singing like Elvis won the day.

Because Professor Higgins never gave up on pursuing his passion to dance and sing on stage with Evis, he provided a grand opportunity for me to experience how genuine acceptance can be loving, lifting and healing.

Jeanie's astute observation of Chris singing "two octaves plus a flat" off key struck me as a brilliant analogy describing the way Chris fits in the world. This phenomenon of Chris hearing music in a different key verifies the different reality he lives in, yet his life resonates with his unique melodious contribution to humanity.

Chris remains faithful to his dream of being a famous singer and still looks forward to the day he will get a call from a Hollywood talent scout. His old cassettes and recorder have been replaced by a cell phone with playlists, and these days he asks me to record him singing so we can post his videos online or send them directly to Hollywood. He carefully watches my fingers to make sure I hit send before concluding each recording session. (Thank you to family members and friends who graciously receive these videos without complaint.)

Everyone in our family continues to be enriched by Chris' passion for music. If you drive past his house to this day, you may be fortunate enough to hear him singing through his bedroom window at the top of his lungs—two octaves plus a flat lower. He is still living his dreams in his own key, as should we all.

LESSON 11

"Bye Bye Bye" To Limiting Beliefs

Throughout Chris' childhood, our family's weekly housecleaning routine was typical and unremarkable until one Saturday morning when everything changed. Chris was about eleven years old, Kathryn ten, Tara nine, and Aubrey was still a baby.

"It isn't fair!" Tara's face grew red as she read the job list I handed her. She leaned past me and looked at the list on my desk for Kathryn. "You give us too many jobs and they're much bigger than what you give Chris."

I replied with my default, *I'm not really listening to you and don't want to argue* defense of, "life isn't always fair." As I reached into my desk drawer for a small post-it note to make Chris' list, Tara continued to argue.

"You treat him like a baby, and he's eleven—two years older than I am!" Tara's voice was strained with frustration because I never conceded to her oft-repeated argument.

"Your list is not too hard for *you*. And the less time we argue, the sooner we'll all be done, and we can go to the beach." I forced a smile. I wished we could all just happily clean our house as if we were Disney princesses prancing around the house singing, "La-dee-da-dee-da!" (I seriously needed a reality check on my expectations!)

Almost every time I handed out checklists for family chores, we had the same argument. Kathryn and Tara handled various jobs depending on our needs, such as the dishes, vacuuming and cleaning. But they knew exactly what was on Chris' small list since it never changed from week to week.

Because he couldn't read, I drew the same three pictures on his list which symbolized simple tasks:

1) wipe off the TV;
2) empty wastebaskets; and
3) pick up the toys in the family room.

"You spoil Chris, and he plays you like a fiddle!" Tara stomped her foot as she walked out of the room to clean the kitchen. ("La-dee-da-dee-da" definitely wasn't in the air that Saturday morning.)

Kathryn walked over to my desk and picked up her own list. "Mom, you know she's right. It isn't fair that we have to do eeeeeverything around here. Chris is much more capable than you treat him. You totally spoil him."

Although Kath had no idea what "doing everything" around the house even looked like, I had to admit she was right about one thing. I spoiled Chris.

Guilty as charged!

How could I not lovingly cater to my cute little Buddy? Whenever I looked into his beautiful blue/grey eyes, I just melted. But, in my defense, Chris clearly wasn't as mature or competent as his younger sisters. He was intellectually functioning at about a kindergarten level—maybe less.

It was hard to know his actual level of understanding since he rarely talked and still relied heavily on sign language. Although he was much better at using signs after years of practice, he used few words and rarely signed complete thoughts. His sisters and I constantly coaxed him to talk with words, but it was much easier for him to move his hands around than to be articulate. (And he didn't have to repeat himself as we tried to decipher his mumbling.) Without clear communication it was hard to know his true capabilities.

My daughters were also right that I expected much more of them than I did of Chris. And I was so grateful that they stepped up to the plate. Kathryn and Tara were like second mothers to Chris and their baby sister, Aubrey.

My lack of time affected the entire family, and I relied heavily on everyone's willingness to help. At that time of my life, I was attending law school at night and over-whelmed by how much study time it required. I was trying to juggle school, work, with my many family responsibilities. I will always appreciate how my husband and daughters rallied to support me through this incredibly challenging time. In addition to being patient with the chaos of our house and my schedule, it took determination and flexibility to get enough quality time with our children. I recall often thinking at the time that I didn't need a therapist half as much as a housekeeper! But finances were too tight considering the cost of law school.

That particular Saturday morning, I had asked more from my daughters than usual. Secretly, I didn't blame them for being upset about the length of their chore lists, but I tried not to let them see the hopeless exhaustion in my eyes. I needed their help to dig out from under all the mess. It was the sort of day when I could barely climb over the mountain of dirty laundry in order to reach the washer and dryer.

Trying to flip the script, I put N'SYNC in the CD player to pump up our work party and bopped to "Bye Bye Bye." I walked upstairs and found Chris watching Saturday morning cartoons. He didn't seem phased when I turned off the TV, handed him cleaning supplies and his list. Pointing to each picture, I reminded him of what they symbolized.

"Eee Hee," was his nonchalant response.

I smiled at Chris and thought how incredibly lucky he was to be so lovingly cared for and to have such wonderful sisters to carry his load. Kath and Tara were attentive and kind to their brother and never spoke a harsh word about him — except when it came to housework.

And so began our usual Saturday morning routine. Kathryn and Tara accepted their unfair lot in life and dutifully went to work. I focused on "mom tasks" and felt contented by our teamwork. We were as happy as we could be—it was as good as it gets. We were functioning like a well-oiled cleaning machine. A cleaner house gave me peace of mind and the kids were happily looking forward to our afternoon at the beach.

Several minutes later I heard the TV playing and walked back into the family room to find Chris watching the very TV he was supposed to be cleaning. The glass cleaner and paper towels were still in the bucket lying next to him, untouched.

"Buddy, you need to finish your jobs before you can watch TV." I feigned a stern voice to cover up how charmed I was by him. He looked so cute sitting crossed legged on the carpet with his head tilted as far back as it could go and his little chin jutting out. He looked like little Lucky, one of the puppies watching TV in *101 Dalmatians.*

"I can't. I hannycat." Chris mumbled in his monotone voice without blinking or taking his eyes off the TV. His matter-of-fact tone of speech claiming himself to be "handicapped" surprised me. I stood motionless and stared at him in disbelief. The aftershock broke some sort of dam in my head and enlightenment flooded my mind.

His sisters were right!

Chris was much smarter than I had ever given him credit for!

I don't know what startled me more. I rarely heard

him even use words, yet he had strung four words together to express a complete thought. And it was the first time I'd ever heard him say "handicapped." I wondered how he knew that word, and why he believed it meant he was incapable of doing household chores.

"Well! The jig is up!" I proclaimed as I walked past him and turned off the TV. "If you are smart enough to offer that crafty argument, you are clearly capable enough to handle more jobs around the house!"

Eventually we all loaded into the car, blasted some Disney tunes and drove to the beach. Everyone had successfully completed their lists—even Chris with extra coaching.

As I sat on the beach watching Chris play in the wet sand at the water's edge, I pondered what more he could be capable of. How had I inadvertently become the mom with too low of expectations for my son?

A small wave rolled in and washed over his small pile of sand and Chris merely leaned back and quietly watched his work melt away. He didn't fight the water or try to dig a trench to protect whatever he was creating from the next tidal surge. Why didn't he seem to care that his pile of sand—his tiny castle—had just washed away? Why didn't he fight to protect what he'd created?

I then realized that Chris was just as accepting and indifferent playing on the beach as he usually was with me. What if I'm washing over him with my perspective about his delimited capabilities? I wondered how many times he hadn't stood up to me and stopped me when I might've been wrong.

Because of Chris' natural tendency to calmly lean back and let things happen to him I knew I needed to not let my—or anyone else's—limiting beliefs about his abilities wash over and diminish him.

I reflected on Chris' silly attempt that morning to persuade me that he was too handicapped to work. If he was intelligent enough to formulate such an argument, then he was clearly capable of handling more challenging chores. *Tara was right! Chris had played me like a fiddle.* I scowled at the thought. *But I was no longer going to be a willing instrument.*

I pondered the significant difference between Chris' IQ—which was under 90—and my own. It had been so easy for me to see right through Chris' silly argument that he was incapable. At this moment of arrogant introspection, I imagined God interrupting me with the words, "You want to talk about IQ differences? You're all handicapped compared to me, and it's silly that one of you thinks you're smarter than any other."

My head jerked back as the imaginary censure exploded through my pretentiousness. I recalled a theory that people use only one-half (or less) of the full potential of our brains which prompted several more insights to wash over me. I realized that egotism—the type of thinking I had just done—was the root cause of some of the worst harms to humanity. Judging others and thinking we are smarter or better is a slippery slope which easily leads to prejudice, self-entitlement, fighting and abuse of power.

I noticed how comparison can obfuscate truth. For example, although I might've demonstrated wisdom in some situations in my life, I hadn't been astute enough to see Chris' actual capabilities. And I hadn't been smart enough to listen to my daughters who could see Chris' true ability more clearly than I had. Who was I to determine one type of intelligence to be more important than another?

Because of my limiting beliefs about Chris' capacity, I had inadvertently become my son's most debilitating handicap. Although I never sought out to hold him back, somehow my mistaken perceptions of him had lowered my expectations and kept him from doing more. My babying him and speaking for him had stalled his growth. I knew that true intelligence would seek to lift others to higher ground and encourage everyone to be the best they can be, rather than limiting their potential.

I don't know how long I was lost in my thoughts as I sat on the beach that afternoon experiencing swelling pride followed by crashing waves of humility and eventually feeling the regret of my mistakes. I committed to myself that day to try to see others from Heaven's view—that no one is smarter or better than anyone else. We each have something to bring to the table and offer each other.

Many things changed in our family that day. I increased my expectations of Chris around the house and although his progress was slow, we celebrated every attempt he made to stretch his ability. Chris learned to set and clear the table, to carry groceries in from the car, to clean out the car and to help put away laundry. Eventually he became capable of bigger jobs such as getting the mail, washing dishes, and taking trash cans out and in.

Chris was clearly not pleased when I pushed him to speak more without signs. He held out in silent protest on many occasions, but I stood my ground. I pretended to misinterpret his signs such as "turn up the music" or "more food" and he'd grunt in disgust.

Although Chris' speech remained difficult to understand, I was tenacious in urging him to leave his comfort zone to practice full sentences to express his thoughts. Instead of dominating meal conversations, his sisters and I asked Chris questions and reminded each other to wait for his answers. We gave him more time to formulate and express his thoughts. And if we allowed for a moment of quiet after Chris spoke, he sometimes even said more.

One day Chris gave his first talk in church. I'll never forget it because we rehearsed together so much that I still have it memorized. He told me what he wanted to say, and I drew pictures to remind him of his own words.

He walked to the pulpit alone and although he was visibly shaking with nerves, he leaned in close to the microphone and didn't hesitate over one mumbled word. Chris looked down at the pictures on his paper and carefully articulated each word, taking time to intentionally look up at the audience as we'd practiced. (My late dad, the Grand something of Toastmasters would have been so proud.)

"Myname...isChrisHiggins. Myfavert...song...is...*I'm uhChild aGod.*"

He continued at a snail's pace, "I...am...happy." (He looked up and smiled as widely as he could.) "I...have... uhfamly." The congregation was quiet and nobody moved—as if they were hanging on his every word. I couldn't take my eyes off Chris as I breathed in the love and acceptance in the silent chapel.

"Aluf...mamom. Aluf madad. Aluf ma sissers. Aluf evbody and you." He looked directly at the audience, pointed to his eye, and crinkled the right side of his face in slow motion to wink.

"Ah...amhappy...God lufsme. Ahn...God lufsyou." He posed with one finger pointed like a gun toward the audience and froze with another large, toothy grin. The audience laughed. (It was his big move.)

After his two minute talk, he looked directly at me with an air of confidence and held his head tall as he said "amen," turned and returned to his seat. If a heart could physically burst with pride, I would've died that day— happily.

After church, our friends and other church members thronged him with congratulations for giving such a great talk. He responded, "yup" to their accolades and nodded his agreement.

As I learned to hold Chris more capable and stayed curious about unexpected possibilities for him, something changed in the way I also saw myself. Previously I had occasionally thought my college goals were too high and unattainable. I had often been overwhelmed and discouraged by so much being required of me on my quest to attend law school while working and raising a large family. I'll never forget the first day of law school when I brought home so many books which I was required to read that semester that I couldn't see over the stack of them on my desk. I sadly thought, *even if I could see over all these books, I'd just see a messy, neglected house. Why do I think I can do this?* Especially when sleep deprived, it was easy to give myself permission to give up and admit, *I can't do it all.* At the beginning of each semester, I had many moments when I sincerely believed I wasn't capable enough. Having a family or a job could legitimately be a handicap in law school.

Thankfully, Professor Higgins showed me the feebleness of my argument. When feeling overwhelmed by life's responsibilities or my lofty goals, I remind myself of Chris' unexpected lesson on the beach that pivotal day. Rather than simply leaning back and letting feelings of hopelessness wash over me and dissolve my dreams or goals, I remember to protect my desires and choose differently by asking myself, "Should I dig a trench, build a wall or what's another way?" If I could hold Chris capable of stretching and doing more, I could expect the same of myself.

Professor Higgins' lesson is for all of us—we are not "hannycat" by our circumstances—including a medical diagnosis, but only by our limiting beliefs about them. We each face challenges or goals which may seem too difficult, but which offer an opportunity to discover how much more we can do than we currently know.

LESSON 12
Listening With Respect To Vulcan Beliefs

C hris *does not* clean his ears when he showers. After months of him refusing my prompting to do so, I took over what should've been a mere routine cleaning behind and around the front recesses of his ears. But this was *not* a simple task and eventually the undertaking turned into a war when Chris was about nine or ten years old and became strong enough to push me away.

I couldn't understand why my teddy bear of a son who trusted me in every other situation, could be so afraid and fought off simple cleanings. I tried everything I could think of to assure and calm him. I asked him why he was afraid and why he fought as aggressively as he did, but his replies were merely incoherent ramblings and angry grunts. I carefully explained to Chris what I was doing, drew pictures, and had one of his sisters demonstrate sitting calmly for the simple cleaning. I even tried offering bribes — nothing helped. Our struggle only became more intense.

I approached ear cleanings with a heavy heart, anxiety, trepidation (and an aspirin), knowing the encounter would become not only a battle of our wits, but also a physical one. Each ear cleaning clash ended the same. After loving, coaxing, begging, pleading, and bribing, I resorted to pinning Chris down with my leg and cleaning his ear with a washcloth as quickly as I could while Chris howled. (I was careful not to hurt him; I just kept him still.)

Chris mastered the art of the warrior's battle scream. It was his most effective strategy to get me to give up—which happened often. But it only prolonged my dread about our next encounter. His shrieks were so loud I felt the need to explain to my neighbors that if they heard terrifying screams coming from my upstairs windows, I was merely cleaning my son's ears. I assured them he was never being harmed and was unjustifiably afraid. On occasion, he and I delivered brownies to our neighbors to apologize and explain. (What a relief they trusted me—*I hoped*—and never called Child Protective Services.)

I postponed each dreaded cleaning for as long as possible because this heartbreaking conflict wounded our otherwise tender, loving relationship. When the cleaning was done, he was angry but quickly forgiving. Yet, no matter my coaxing, he wouldn't explain why he was so afraid.

Finally, one day a miraculous resolution happened.

During one of Chris' routine medical visits with our favorite family doctor, I pleaded for help.

"Doctor Lacomb, will you please explain to Chris that I need to clean his ears once in a while, and tell him not to fight me? I've tried to convince him that I won't hurt him, but he screams in fear and fights me every time. The fights are pretty bad, and they break my heart, but I don't know what else I can do to convince him that he's safe." As I further explained the painful details about our cleaning bouts, I caught a glimpse of Chris hunched over, defiantly folding his arms and scowling at me as he sat on the exam table.

Here we go! I thought, *here comes his stubborn defiance. He won't listen and nothing will ever be resolved.*

Doctor Lacomb listened but didn't respond to me. Instead, he turned and looked Chris squarely in his eyes. In a kind voice he asked, "Chris, why don't you let your mom clean your ears?"

Chris sat up straight, threw his hands in the air and exclaimed, "Doctor NaCoy, ev'y tine my mom cleans ma ears—she pulls ma ears. I gonna get…Vulcan ears…like Spock!"

My eyebrows raised, my eyes popped open wide, and my jaw dropped as I stared in disbelief at Chris. I was shocked to hear him speak so articulately. He talked slowly and paused often, but he spoke in complete sentences. And why did Chris refer to him as Dr. McCoy from Star Trek? Where did that come from? But apparently Chris believed he was talking to the real Dr. McCoy. Rarely had I seen Chris make such an articulate, passionate and animated argument. I was stunned and speechless.

Our doctor didn't seem phased by the absurdity of Chris' comments. He squared his shoulders, took a breath and slowly nodded receipt of the information.

Without breaking eye contact with Chris, he calmly and slowly explained, "Chris, I'm not Dr. McCoy, but I know who he is—and Mr. Spock. But I *am* a doctor, so you can trust me when I say, *you cannot get* Vulcan ears just by pulling on your ears."

Chris stared at the doctor in silence as if he were carefully weighing the doctor's advice. His passion had evaporated, and his shoulders relaxed as he studied our doctor's face. Dr. Lacomb waited for Chris' reply without breaking eye contact. He barely blinked.

I felt like I was in a time warp. I sat frozen in stunned disbelief staring at Chris and Dr. Lacomb. Only my head moved as I looked back and forth from the doctor to Chris.

After a moment, Dr. Lacomb continued in his same matter-of-fact tone. "You have to have a Vulcan parent to get Vulcan ears."

I started to think I was somehow transported to an alternate universe.

"Now, I can see that your mom is not a Vulcan." Dr. Lacomb continued, "Is your father a Vulcan?"

I turned my head slowly to look at Chris curious as to how he was going to respond—it was as if I was watching a movie in slow motion.

Chris looked down at his legs taking his time to fully contemplate the question of whether his father was a Vulcan. (As if he needed to think about it!) I thought it was funny it took him more than a second to respond, but I was still too stunned to laugh—and our doctor certainly wasn't laughing.

"Umhhh...nooooo," Chris finally answered.

"Then, you can never get Vulcan ears," our doctor assured him. Dr. Lacomb then turned, looked directly at me and added, "and from now on, your mom won't ever pull on your ears when she cleans them."

It took a moment for me to ground myself—or in this case, come back to earth. But my dumbfounded gaze quickly turned into a jubilant grin as I blurted, "Yes! I promise!"

Still shaking off my surprise over the surreal conversation I just witnessed, I glanced around the room as if expecting a Hollywood crew from Candid Camera to appear from the corners or tall cabinets. And when they didn't, I thought *what a shame no one else witnessed that! Nobody will ever believe I was a part of this entertaining consultation!*

"Do we have a deal?" Doctor Lacomb asked Chris.

"Uh-huh." Chris smiled with a thumbs up. And just like that, in warp speed, our ear cleaning war was over, and peace returned to our section of the galaxy.

I learned much from this other-worldly encounter. First, doctors are not only heroes, but they also can be Trekkies—which is so cool. As the doctor left the room, I winked and smiled at him with sincere admiration and gratitude. He maintained his professional demeanor and only granted me a slight nod of his head, as if acknowledging that his creative problem solving had merely been all in a day's work.

After that day, I never again needed to engage in a fight with Chris to clean his ears. I was careful not to touch his earlobes which Chris noticed and appreciated. We made no "Bones"[2] about our past battles, and trust returned to our relationship. Chris had been right about one thing—previously when cleaning his ears, I always pulled on them—albeit only slightly. I don't know why I did that. I did it without thinking.

Perhaps I should have noticed clues because I knew Chris loved Star Trek movies. I could recite most of the movie lines from memory after hearing them constantly playing in the background in our home for a few years.

All those years, I'd never realized Chris and I had been fighting over completely different issues and beliefs. I thought the problem was simply dirty ears and judged his response to be overly dramatic or stubborn. My reality was simple—the task needed to be done, and it was merely one small task on my long list of things to do.

---

[2] Dr. McCoy's nickname (if you're not a Trekkie).

Chris' reality was light years apart from mine. He worried about something much more significant—he feared being permanently disfigured. Of course he would fight!

Neither time nor force had resolved our differences. No matter his age or how many times I repeated my assurances to not hurt him, he never gave in. And I never backed down either. As long as I was stronger than he was and could pin him down, I prevailed.

I don't believe we ever would've resolved our battles without our doctor's extraordinary help. All those years, I would've never guessed—as it was highly illogical—our ear cleaning conflict would require intergalactic intervention.

I've never forgotten the brilliant result Dr. Lacomb achieved from listening with sincere curiosity. In my defense, I *had* asked Chris many times why he fought me over cleaning his ears. But his indecipherable mumblings never offered any understandable explanation. Although I remember Chris occasionally talking—in fractured speech—about Vulcans or Vulcan ears, he never brought it up when we talked about cleaning his ears or while engaged in combat.

Or did he? In recalling the conversations Chris and I shared about Vulcans, I only half-heartedly listened or participated due to my lack of genuine interest "to boldly go where no one has gone before." Our past Star Trek conversations usually ended with me laughing, smiling, or absent-mindedly agreeing with him. I'd never been a sci-fi fan, but I would've remembered hearing something unusual like being afraid of getting Vulcan ears.

After further reflection, I must also admit that I didn't listen to Chris with the same respect Dr. Lacomb had. Maybe I dismissed Chris' prior outbursts as childish, angry rantings. On the other hand, perhaps Chris never expressed his real worries. I wondered if it was because he hadn't trusted me to be receptive to his truth—his reality. My erroneous judgements of him—that he was angry, scared, stubborn or unable to understand me—showed disrespect and could have been what blocked his trust in me. Perhaps, that was why Chris didn't even try to communicate his fear to me of having Vulcan ears.

Professor Higgins and our favorite Trekkie, Dr. Lacomb, both deserve credit for teaching me a powerful lesson—how respectful listening helps to resolve conflicts. But for Professor Higgins' extraordinary imagination, I wouldn't have enjoyed the opportunity to "beam up" so adeptly to this new level of understanding and awareness.

Resolving our ear cleaning war began with the simple question "why?" Being interested and respectful enough to ask the why in ongoing conflicts can uncover core values and beliefs necessary to help understand each other. Capt. Kirk understood this and wisely said, "There's no such thing as the 'unknown'—only things temporarily hidden, temporarily not understood."

Professor Higgins taught me how trust is critically interconnected with effective listening. Perhaps it was because our doctor looked Chris directly in his eyes when asking his questions. Maybe it was just because the white doctor's coat shouted, "trust me," but it more likely was because of the feeling in the room created by Dr. Lacomb's genuine curiosity. Because he trusted his listener and he felt respected by him, Chris opened up and shared his sincere truths.

Dr. Lacomb first established common ground without regard to how unbelievable Chris' statements were. Before responding to the accuracy of Chris' beliefs, he simply acknowledged knowing Dr. McCoy and Spock. Chris' Vulcan theories weren't received with disbelief or laughter. Rather, Chris was respectfully listened to with acceptance. As Mr. Spock once said, "There are always possibilities."

Some people's truths may turn out to be similar to Vulcan beliefs which are highly illogical from an earthly perspective. When listening to others with curiosity, respect and understanding, solutions *are* possible—even for Vulcan-type issues.

I'm now a convert to sci-fi through all my Trekkie teachers, including Professor Higgins. I've learned how listening with sincere respect, rather than minimizing, laughing at, or otherwise dismissing unconventional beliefs can make all the difference in reaching everyone's ultimate final frontier—the hinterland of peace.

May we all listen to each other with curiosity, respect and acceptance for all beliefs. In so doing, may we all live long and prosper.

LESSON 13

Patience Is Unconditional Love

I was born impatient. Throughout my life and most of Chris' life, I have lived in a constant mindset of looking forward to the next best thing. Despite recognizing that we can't have everything all at once, I wanted to be smarter, wealthier and more accomplished—right now. It's taken a lot of energy to conceal my impatience with anyone or anything slowing me down. Everyone has heard the adage "patience is a virtue," but I had to find out the hard way.

I noticed and admired people with a zen lifestyle and wanted to develop the mind-set to *be* a woman of patience. Although a part of me thought I'd never nail down this trait, my back up plan was hoping I would naturally wax more patient with age.

I was wrong. During college and early years of my career while raising children, I didn't put much effort into practicing calmness and tolerance. Because frankly, I didn't have time for fanciful matters. I noticed how my unreasonable expectations caused my relationships to suffer. Eventually, it became clear that patience isn't gleaned simply by aging; I needed to learn how to shift to a whole new state of *being*. I wanted to change but didn't know how. Self-help books, observing others and seeking advice offered strategies to pattern new habits, but knowledge alone wasn't enough to transform me into *being* patient. Luckily, Professor Higgins came into my life to eventually teach me a thing or two about accepting what is, loving others enough to accept them as they are, and the need to be fully present.

Chris moves through life in slow motion. He operates at the pace of a sloth—an adorable sloth, but too sluggish for my tastes. In his early years, I gnashed my teeth and endured his plodding pace. But as he grew older, he resisted anything he didn't want to do by going limp or slowing down even more.

Chris' "DMV-sloth" pace posed a real problem to our everyday family life when his siblings were still at home. As a parent with a demanding job, I worked long hours with little time to get everything done for my children and home and sleep deprivation was my constant companion. Between my job and my children, I craved just one more minute of sleep every morning, and frantically rushed to get one more thing done before leaving for work. I needed Chris to move quickly before school or his day program, but he didn't care about my need for "just one more." Although I detested being late, we often were, and my nagging went unheeded.

How did an expert multi-tasker such as I happily co-exist with a dedicated single-tasker who lived as a master of slowness? Easy answer—I did everything. For instance, when he didn't want to go to school and moved at his slowest pace, I dressed Chris. It was a pathetic, molly-coddling sight to behold. Chris sat in his bedroom chair as I placed his shirt over his head, with him raising one arm at a time. He stood up for a few seconds as I pulled up his pants and fell back into his chair for me to put on his shoes and socks. I even shaved him with one hand while combing his hair with the other. When his teachers learned of my enabling ways, his annual goals (for years) became "dress yourself." The teacher would read it aloud during school conferences as they glared at me across the table. Clearly, they were actually *my* annual goals.

I wish I could share some enlightened parenting advice about how I resolved this, but taking over Chris' tasks or bribing him were the only successful ways to get him quickly dressed and in the car. Chris' love language was treats and he spoke this language fluently. Chocolate bribes evolved from M&Ms as a small child to fun-sized Snickers™ bars as an adult, but they worked! It seems I had turned into the Titanic Mom of what not to do—and please don't report me to his current job coach and counselors, but occasionally I still dress him when we're late.

When I wasn't doing everything for Chris to meet

time deadlines, I was constantly encouraging him to move. (I'm sure he would call it nagging.) The underlying problem of how we could peacefully function together with such different agendas plagued us for years and made us both unhappy.

In a quintessential scene, Chris stands at the top of the stairs and I'm at the bottom trying to get him out the door.

"Hurry Chris, go fast!" I've said hundreds of times. I stand in my regular post at the front door shouting this encouragement three...four...twelve times before he drifts toward me. Because my badgering always creates tension, I alternatively interject pleas of, "We're not going to make it on time" or "I'm going to lose my job if I'm late." Other than bribing him with food, I didn't know what to do. Chris didn't care about being late. He didn't understand the concept of "on time" or why it is important.

Chris never changed, but one evening when Chris was about twenty-five years old, something changed in me. We were leaving to go to a movie when my frustration with his slow pace turned to laughter. I watched Chris lift each leg and slowly lower it to the next step down as I yelled my usual plea from the bottom of the stairs, "Please Buddy, go fast! We're going to miss the beginning of the show!"

"I hate dat word 'gofast!'" Chris mumbled loud enough to make sure I heard. To make matters worse he stopped moving in order to complain. (Walking and talking at the same time is a skill set he doesn't always employ.) Chris stood on the stairway staring at me with an exaggerated frown. He slowly lifted his finger and pointed to his frown to make sure I knew of his sadness. If I allowed his drama to go on another thirty seconds, he probably would've produced a tear to show how bullied he felt. If I weren't lost in internal giggling over his charming charade, I might've been duped into feeling sorry for Chris.

His lack of knowing "go fast" to actually be two words symbolized the vast difference between us. The reminder softened me to smile and in a quiet voice say, "But I love 'go fast' My Buddy. It gets us to the movie in time to get a treat and see the beginning." I walked up the stairs to meet him, took his hand and kissed it.

"I'm sorry you think I'm yelling at you when I'm trying to hurry you." My apology softened his scowl—or perhaps it was the promised treat that did the trick. While walking slowly down the stairs together I pondered the vastly different worlds Chris and I live in. He didn't understand my anxieties or know how well his life worked when getting to places on time.

Going to a movie or out to eat were Chris' favorite pastimes, but I preferred staying home whenever possible because public restrooms posed a worry once he became old enough to want to use the men's restroom instead of the women's with me. I'll never forget the pivotal day he pointed to the men's room sign with one hand and with a thumb pointing to his chest, he declared, "man." He pulled away from me. I quashed my desire to grab him but watched him saunter inside—alone. Every time he moseys into the men's room, a slight sickening fear seeps into my gut with the worry he might be harmed. Chris has proven to be exemplary in washing his hands, one finger at a time. He takes so long in the men's room I often wonder if he's been assaulted or kidnapped. At times I've resorted to asking a kind stranger to go in and see if Chris is safe. He's never changed his preference for the men's room and I'm constantly afraid he's in danger. I still pace back and forth wondering if, after a few minutes I should yell, "Are you ok in there, Chris?"

During family trips involving extensive walking such as going to theme parks or getting through an airport, one family member always held Chris' hand and pulled him along. At theme parks, it took one to pull and another to push to keep him moving to the next ride. I endured humiliating stares from onlookers alerted by Chris' protests of exaggerated moans and struggles to pull his hand loose. I wanted to yell out assurances, "No, we're *not* kidnapping this boy" or "don't worry, I'm a loving mother," or "yes, this is as hard as it looks" and "yes, he stops frequently and just won't move!"

Many theme park excursions and an almost missed flight later, it finally occurred to me that I could push Chris in a wheelchair faster than he walked! Everyone in the family celebrated the first time we zipped through an airport pushing Chris and arrived at our gate with plenty of time—without having to be at the airport an extra hour early. And our family finally got to experience the Happiest Place on Earth without misery!

I'm chagrined to admit that following the wheelchair epiphany I discovered his extremely flat feet and hip issues caused him pain during extended periods of walking or standing. Lethargy wasn't his only issue, and I felt terrible not discovering this sooner.

This taught me to pause and examine things more closely—my concern was getting Chris to match my pace. He needed to move within the time constraints of a world that isn't typically scheduled to accommodate him. But by doing so, I had missed something that his physical pace was broadcasting. We addressed his pain and physical issues, and to this day the wheelchair is Chris' favorite ride at theme parks. He grins and practically runs to the wheelchair line knowing it's the ride with the shortest wait time and his sore feet will be spared from painful standing, walking, or being pulled and pushed all day. (Thank you, Disneyland™ for providing wheelchairs to people with all types of disabilities.)

Despite feeling tyrannized by his time delays, I genuinely admire Chris' ability to live in the now. Being in tune with his senses and prioritizing happiness allows him to be a peaceful and loving guy. And Chris genuinely wants everyone to experience happiness too. The flipside of this means he does not react well when anyone appears upset. He wants everyone to be happy and he misinterprets emotions such as anxiety, frustration, or stress to be anger. If he thinks the anger is directed at him, his sadness slows him down further or shuts him down completely. (It's a guilt trap!) When the tension of being pushed to "go fast" makes him sad I feel guilty, and I tend to overcompensate to cheer him up—and relieve my guilt. For many years this cycle of dysfunction repeated like clockwork whenever I yelled or had exasperation in my voice.

My task-oriented manner of taking care of Chris remedied most of the tension between us. Outwardly, we were happier, but I was worn out. I knew my impatience, rather than Chris' slow pace, created the genesis of our problem. In truth, I genuinely wanted to *be* patient. With renewed determination I studied self-help books for a secret formula to transform myself into a model of forbearance; I memorized mantras such as "I feel calm, safe and grounded," and "I surrender to the festival of life." I practiced new habits, but inside I was the same. By the time I was fifty, I could clearly see the collapse of any hope that I would graciously age into the tolerant and peaceful woman I wanted to become. I consoled myself by rationalizing that an extremely productive and ambitious person could inherently be high strung and impatient. With little faith left that I could change, I decided to accept myself as I was and give up on trying to *be* patient. I willed myself to stay tranquil and soldiered on.

My pretense of peace was all I had until one Saturday afternoon when Professor Higgins and his brother, Jared, both presented an effective lesson to me.

Chris seemed happy as he sat at the kitchen table waiting for his favorite chocolate chip cookies to finish baking. We basked in the warmth from the cookie aroma and talked about the next movie he wanted to see. Jared walked in and drew in a loud, deep breath.

"Mm-hmm." Jared poured himself a tall glass of milk and sat down next to Chris. They gave each other a 'thumbs up' and beamed with anticipation.

"Those cookies smell great and just what I need after a hard day at work," Jared said. It made me happy to see the smiles on their faces. When I placed the plate of warm cookies on the table between them, we noticed Chris eyeing Jared's glass of milk with longing.

"I have milk?" Chris asked Jared.

"Help yourself Buddy." Jared gestured to the gallon of milk still sitting on the counter. He wasn't annoyed. In a genuinely caring way, Jared supported his brother when appropriate, but they were both in their late twenties and Jared didn't baby Chris.

Chris' stare lingered on Jared's glass. Without getting up he picked up a large cookie and looked towards me. Jared and I both knew Chris's gaze hoped to elicit sympathy from me to solve his problem.

"I'm not sharing my glass of milk with you," Jared firmly declared.

He quickly turned to me. "Mom, you know I hate sharing food with anyone and especially not drinks. Chris is capable of pouring himself a glass of milk."

I nodded. Jared's words were not surprising as he is my most germophobic child. I didn't doubt his sincerity in encouraging Chris to help himself. Of course, Chris could pour his own glass of milk. Not babying Chris was the right thing to do.

But while Jared still faced me, I saw Chris dunk his cookie in the glass of milk behind Jared's back. My eyes widened and I gritted my teeth, expecting a tense scene to ensue. Jared saw the expression on my face and spun around just in time to see Chris pull his soggy cookie and milk-drenched fingers out of Jared's glass. I held my breath and waited for Jared's reaction. Jared calmly stood up, marched to the cupboard to get a new glass and filled it with fresh milk.

"You won that one Buddy, but I'll get you next time!" Jared sternly warned (but with a grin).

"Hee Hee!" Chris smiled from ear to ear exposing a mouthfull of cookie.

A wave of peaceful energy swept the room. I smiled at Jared. "I so admire how you stay calm and never seem to get mad at Chris." I nodded with respect. "I don't know how you do it. I wish I had your patience."

Jared took a large bite and enjoyed the swallow. "It's not patience. It's unconditional love."

I didn't quite grasp what he meant but admired his

unflappable manner. He picked up another cookie and stared at it, as if it were speaking to him. Then he said, "Maybe they're one and the same."

Jared's words stayed with me. I didn't doubt their truth because he seemed genuinely at peace with Chris' mischievous act. I felt the contentment and love which filled the room. Instead of Jared correcting Chris or turning the incident into a teaching moment, as I expected, he chose peace.

As I pondered the cookie-dunking experience, lessons began to unfold expanding my core beliefs about my ability to *be* patient. I reasoned, if patience naturally flows from unconditional love, then it must include accepting others as they are without an intent to force my expectations on them or otherwise try to change them. By accepting this truth, I could see how genuine patience is not achieved by strategies and sheer determination.

Somehow, a light switch turned on inside me. When existing in a state of impatience I lost opportunities to be more present and aware of what's going on in my son's mind (or anyone else's) rather than focusing just on the task of the moment. This was why I didn't see important things such as Chris' painful flat feet and hip issues early on. My tendency to push myself to accomplish too much in too little time and holding the same expectation for others had always been my problem to resolve, not others or my son's. It's never been about Chris being too slow, but about my unwillingness to let go of my agenda.

How would it be if I loved my children in a way—just as they are with their differences? What if I respected their uniqueness without focusing on how they should improve or change? And, what if I gave Chris (as well as others) the benefit of the doubt that his intentions weren't to harm or annoy others? Chris really had no bad motive when dunking the cookie—he was thinking only of himself. Pondering these questions and giving my children the benefit of the doubt allowed space for change and more kindness in our family.

As I tried out my new theories on my children, their quick and inspiring responses amazed me. For example, when Aubrey changed her college major for the fourth time, I told her that I would no longer push her to graduate, but that I trusted her to know what was best for her—that she didn't need to make decisions based on my expectations. Through tears, she thanked me for believing in her. (But I set a deadline to end my donations.)

I had previously tried to compliment all my kids about their individual traits. Now, because I acknowledged their ability to become their best selves without the hinderance of my expectations, they finally seemed to believe my sincere admiration.

Understanding how unconditional love and patience are related has been a game changer in all my relationships, but particularly with Chris. Becoming accountable for my perspective of his slow pace being a problem seemed to make our conflict disappear. My prior opinion had clearly not been based on acceptance, but rather my judgment of what his appropriate pace should be. Who is to say who is right and who is wrong, who is good and who is bad? After all, the tortoise won the proverbial race against the hare.

Chris' way of being, including his slow pace, has been a significant gift to me—the catalyst which finally taught me more than books could. I learned not only what patience looks like, but also what it felt like. And I witnessed, firsthand, the positive impact it had on others.

Although it took years for Chris' teachings to sink in (and I'm still practicing), I could not think of a more perfect package to present this lesson to me. I had given up several times in my life on whether I could transform on this issue. Without full acceptance of Chris as he is, my frustration with his pace could have remained front and center throughout our entire relationship until one of us died—even perhaps beyond death because if he had died, I probably would condemn myself for not creating more peace when we were alive.

My unhappiness and exhaustion resulting from years of trying to control others or change them humbled me enough to finally be able to receive the lesson Professor Higgins offered. Because I could never walk away from my beloved Chris, I ultimately learned how love is not only the impetus to transform, but also the key.

I've learned to welcome daily opportunities to love Professor Higgins as he is, not who I expect him to be.

Since I accept Chris' interpretation of yelling to be anger in his perspective, I try to be present about the tone of my voice and limit it. If I'm anxious about anything, including leaving the house on time, I try to walk to him, use a soft voice and gently touch him so he feels loved.

When staying present, I expect him to be slow, accept it and even have a little fun with it. For instance, the other day we were at a truck stop and he needed to use the men's room. As he walked away, in lieu of my usual fear and pacing routine, I called out, "I'm just going to wait here for you and sip on your soda until you return." His head swiveled and he looked at me with alarm.

I held up his drink. "Here's to a fast restroom trip!" He turned and darted inside. A few short minutes later he hustled back to me with his hands still soapy—he hadn't wasted any time drying his hands. He took his cup and lifted it high to see how much of his soda remained.

"You were so fast I didn't have time to drink any!" I smiled. Chris grinned and gave me a big bear hug.

It has been many years since the day when Chris walked down the stairs complaining of his hatred for the word, "gofast." While he is still an adorable sloth, I'm more at peace with his timeframes. His speed has never changed but getting to places together has been more fun. Not simply because we are older and wiser, but because I learned how to choose a new state of *being*.

LESSON 14

Being The Star Of The Show

When Chris was about twenty-three, he was lucky to join Care-Rite Vocational Services, a company providing work experience and training in life skills for people with intellectual and developmental disabilities. Chris enjoyed his various jobs and adored his coaches. But the highlight of his Care-Rite career was participating in their theater group, which is well-known in our hometown for its annual musical performances. Chris and his fellow actors feel like A-List celebrities due to their professional costuming, sets and sold out crowds. Chris knew it wasn't Hollywood, but it was certainly close!

One afternoon, I picked Chris up after auditions for *Beauty and the Beast*. He yanked the car door open and practically jumped as he got in the car. He proudly announced with a big grin, "I am da star of da show!"

"What?" I caught his contagious smile and asked, "do you mean you're going to be Gaston or the Beast? You got the lead role?"

"Yup!" Chris didn't quite answer my questions but pointed to his exaggerated smile. "I am star of da show."

"Oh, Buddy, you're so lucky! You must be Gaston, the handsome brute!"

"Yup!" Chris said again as he rummaged through his beloved Disney CDs to play on our 1980's car stereo. Being the star in a Disney musical was his dream come true and we celebrated all the way home by singing our hearts out.

He walked into the kitchen later while I was making dinner and asked, "You buy me shirt? I am da star ofda show."

"What do you mean?" I noticed the earnest look in his eyes.

"I am star of da show."

"Do you want me to buy a shirt for you with the words 'I am the star of the show?'" I asked. He nodded eagerly with a big grin. Usually I could read his mind, but I was puzzled and a bit put off by his desire to be so pompous.

"Oh no, Buddy, that would be showing off." I ignored his slumped shoulders and exaggerated frown and giggled over what a drama king he could be when he didn't get what he wanted. I dried my hands and touched his shoulder so he could look at me and see my earnestness. "When you really *are* the star of the show, you can't brag about it. It would be rude to all your friends. You don't want to rub it in that *you are the star,* and they aren't. You agree, don't you?"

Chris's furrowed brow and pouty mouth barely moved as he grumbled, "I am star of da show." As usual, my sage advice didn't get through to him.

"Well, we don't want others to feel bad about their roles in the show, Buddy. You don't want to look like you're more important. You don't want to hurt anyone's feelings, and it's better to be polite than important." I ended our one-sided conversation with a kiss on Chris's cheek and called the family to dinner.

I avoided looking at Chris through the first part of dinner, pretending not to notice his melodramatic frown and downcast look. Finally, his sister Tara could tolerate his misery no longer and begged him to share his feelings.

Chris raised his hands in exasperation. "I am da star of da show," Chris grumbled. "I need da shirt." With a concealed smirk and partial eyeroll, I shared Chris's great news. I repeated—for Chris' benefit—the wise and polite reasoning behind my refusal to let him be self-aggrandizing about his role as Gaston in the upcoming play.

Everyone cheered their congratulations to Chris, but his misery was unaffected and he grumbled something about me ruining his life. His brother, Jared, tried to get my back by assuring Chris, "famous actors never wear clothes which announce their star status—they don't like being noticed in public."

"Hulk Hogan does." Chris's persuasive argument made us all laugh.

I dodged his further requests several more times before tucking him into bed that night. "You buy me shirt?" His last words as I turned off the light pierced my enabling heart. I wanted to give in but knew it wasn't the right thing to do.

"Trust me, Buddy. Real stars of the show fly under the radar." I heard my mother's voice come out of me when I added, "that's the polite and classy way to be." I missed her and smiled at the thought that I never fully appreciated her advice when she was alive.

I welcomed the chance to teach Chris about social manners, but he is a champion in the art of perseveration. Something shifted in me as I began to listen to him with my heart.

"I *am* star of *da show*." Chris said again with fervor before I left for work the next morning. Well, it *is* one of our family's favorite shows, I reasoned to myself as I drove. And we should probably celebrate this achievement in his off-Broadway career of landing a lead role!

"I am *da star* of da show," Chris reminded me again when I tucked him into bed the next night. I held the line, but thought it was astonishing that Chris landed a lead role with many songs and lines, considering his speech difficulties. I wondered whether the directors were just being nice to him and had to admit that this play might be his only opportunity to act in a starring role.

"I *am* dastar of the show," he grumbled under his breath at breakfast the next day. I kissed him goodbye and ignored his furrowed brow. But inside I couldn't let it go. What other time in Chris' life would he be able to live out his dreams of being a tall and handsome brute like Gaston?

I ordered the custom shirt.

I just didn't have it in me to put a damper on Chris' joy of living out his Hollywood dreams. And if the other cast members never saw the shirt, what could be the harm? I told him I ordered the shirt but insisted that he couldn't wear it outside of the house until after the play was over.

The day the shirt arrived Chris greeted me at the door wearing it when I came home from work. He pushed his chest out, pointed to the words on the shirt and bounced up and down in a happy dance.

"I know, Buddy. You *are* the star of the show, and I'm proud of you! But remember, don't wear your new shirt on Tuesdays to play practice. It is ONLY to be worn in private." He gave me a grateful, long bear hug which made me feel that all would be well in our world.

Chris wanted to wear his new shirt the next day, the day after, and the day after that—in fact, it was the only shirt he wanted to wear every day, but I held the line. The next Tuesday morning I was relieved when everything seemed back to normal as I left for work and saw him wearing his usual gaudy WWE T-shirt.

Later that afternoon when I entered the auditorium to pick up Chris after play practice, I stopped short. I could feel the heat of both anger and guilt surge through me when I saw him across the room wearing the new shirt. I yelled out to get his attention. He turned and started to walk toward me, but when he paused several times to show his shirt to friends along his route, my eyes rolled in harsh judgment. He smiled, gave a little shimmy and pointed to the words on his shirt. The more animated he looked, the more I shrunk in humiliation—the obnoxious shirt was clearly a mom fail.

My clenched jaw began to loosen as I watched his friends pat him on the back, give him a "thumbs-up" or offer congratulations. My heart softened with gratitude for being so lucky that my son gets to be surrounded by people who were accepting, supportive and non-judgmental. Still, I suffered enough embarrassment for both of us and secretly hoped most of his friends couldn't read.

During the months leading up to the play, Chris never let us forget his starring role. The soundtrack to *Beauty and the Beast* played during every car ride with Chris loudly and proudly singing along. He cherished his new stardom and wore his new favorite shirt in public whenever it was clean (and sometimes when it wasn't). Chris couldn't be dissuaded from approaching random strangers and announcing his star status while pointing to his shirt. I covered up his boastfulness by explaining Chris's shirt as advertising their upcoming community theater production and describing how to get tickets.

The day Chris handed me the list of clothing needed for his costume—a white shirt, brown pants, and suspenders—I was bewildered. With the myriad of scenes involving Gaston, I assumed the costume list would be much longer. There had to be some sort of mistake.

The next morning I called Steven, the Care-Rite manager, and explained the mix up in Chris' clothing list. His response surprised me, "That's right, LeFou only has this one costume."

"Um, what do you mean?" I asked. "Chris said he is playing Gaston."

"No," Steven assured me. "Chris is playing LeFou."

I bit my lower lip and drew a breath. "Um, we may have a problem. Chris has been telling us for months that he's playing Gaston. He has been practicing all the songs and is beyond proud to be the star. You may have seen the obnoxious shirt which he forced me to buy—the one printed with the words, 'the star of the show.'"

Steven laughed, "Yea, Chris showed me his shirt. He is such a jokester!"

Being neither amused nor pacified, I pushed further. "Seriously, it's all he talks about. I'm *sure* he thinks he's playing Gaston. Someone needs to break the news to Chris—and he's going to be heartbroken. I don't think I can do it."

"But Chris knows he's playing LeFou," Steven insisted. "I've been working on his part with him during practices. There's no problem. Trust me."

I was dumbstruck. We hung up after I thanked Steven, but I was more bewildered than ever. Quite opposite of the handsome—even studly—Gaston, LeFou is his obese, dorky sidekick with a large pink nose. I heard myself moan as I slowly shook my head. How could Chris be so out of touch with reality to not even know his character? Even after months of practice? He couldn't have been playing a trick on me—he was clearly proud to be the star. My confusion was overcome by fear of how the hard news would shatter his acting dreams.

Just before bedtime, I sat down on the couch next to Chris, drew in a deep breath, and explained in a soft, slow voice, "My Buddy, I spoke with Steven today. You may be confused about your part in the play."

Chris said nothing and just looked at me with a blank stare. "You're not Gaston in the play, Buddy. I'm still very proud of you, but someone else gets to be the star of the show this time. Maybe you'll be the star of the next show."

"Whaaat?" Chris looked confused.

I put my hand on his back to comfort him. "Buddy, you're not playing Gaston. You are LeFou, Gaston's best friend. He isn't really the star of the show." Hoping to bolster his self-confidence I added, "but he is funny and cute and a great singer—like you." I smiled with all the gentleness and kindness I could muster.

"Hmh," Chris grunted without emotion. "I am da star of da show."

I stared at Chris and struggled to find something to say

that could resolve his reality gap. I had nothing.

With a hug I simply assured him he would always be a star to me. When tucking Chris into bed later that night, I avoided any mention of the play and left his room with no resolution—only a futile hope things might somehow turn out OK.

Over the final weeks of play practice, nothing changed. Chris seemed happy when he mentioned his play and I followed his cue, bit my tongue and smiled to mask the sorrow only a parent understands when expecting a child's dreams to be shattered in a public display.

By opening night, I still hadn't overcome my worries about Chris being disappointed. I planned for the whole family to go out for ice cream after the play, thinking it would take all of us to lift Chris' spirits.

I sat through the beginning of the play, shifting in my seat wondering what Chris was thinking when the other actor—who was actually cast as Gaston—was singing all those songs we had rehearsed in the car. I somewhat expected Chris to burst onto the stage and try to steal the role of Gaston. What a relief that my imaginary fear never became a reality.

Finally, Chris dressed in his nerdy LeFou costume, made his grand appearance. With a thumb under each suspender, a smirk on his face and a hop in his step, he bounded across the stage. I was stunned! I had never seen him hop or look so agile! He was larger than life as he performed—as if he really was the star of the show.

He owned that stage and as he did, he schooled me!

After his first line, he turned to face the audience, posed with a confident smile, eyes wide and head held high. He waited. A lone cheer from his brother broke the awkward silence. Someone began cueing his next line from behind the side curtain, but Chris wouldn't move or speak. He put his right hand up as if to block the cue, stretched his head a little taller, and waived his other hand like a musical conductor to encourage the audience to applaud. Some politely clapped, but it wasn't enough for Chris. Showing off a huge, toothy grin, Chris then waved both arms to encourage more. Only after the audience's generous response with hoots and cheers would he continue his lines.

Eventually, the audience learned to applaud Chris on cue. Every time he walked on stage—even when in the background or in a group—the audience erupted into cheers and clapping. If they failed, he quickly reminded them with the wave of his hands. He welcomed and absorbed the audience's adoration by posing—sometimes awkwardly in the middle of a scene—with both of his arms extended, as if offering everyone a big bear hug.

Chris hijacked the star role and worked the audience that night with exceptional talent. By the end of the play, his siblings were horse from screaming for Chris while I slowly shook my head in disbelief and massaged away the discomfort in my cheeks from grinning too long.

During the final curtain call when LeFou majestically

marched on stage, the screams and cheers were deafening. With tears in my eyes, I looked around to see everyone laughing, grinning, and eagerly applauding Chris as he proudly nodded his head, held out his arms and slowly took his bow. It was as if I had watched a play entitled *LeFou—as told by Beauty & The Beast*.

Afterwards, I watched Chris with admiration as he lingered in the auditorium to autograph playbills. Aubrey and Jared ran to give him a pen and help him work the crowd. A few people even stood in line for his signature! Charmed by Chris' confidence, his fans kept giving him more. While waiting for Chris, I studied the face of my other son whom I had recently adopted and pondered his own self-confidence. He had passed through many significant challenges in his life, including the death of his mother, and struggled to believe in his true self-worth. Then the thought of how I dealt with pride flashed through my mind. Instantly I decided everyone in the family would get a shirt for Christmas printed with, "I am the star of the show."

I became a different mom from that moment forward.

I know some people will simply think I over-indulged Chris and taught him to make everything about himself. Was it indulging to order the custom shirt for Chris to support his dream of being the star of a Disney musical? I used to think so.

However, Professor Higgins taught me how enrolling others into our lives is more than simply garnering support or having a "center of the universe" mentality—it creates powerful emotional connections which can expand to elevate all human life.

His desire for his "star of the show" shirt wasn't about being the center of the universe or thinking he was better than the other actors. It was about connecting with others at such an emotional level that they would not only accept his dreams, but also enjoy the fulfillment of those dreams along with him. Because of this connection, his enrollment of others into his life drew out increased love and encouragement for Chris from me, his siblings, his fellow actors and the entire audience.

Chris doesn't assume people will judge him unfairly; he simply enjoys being happy and freely shares it. Because he trusted in the generosity of his audience, Chris wasn't the only one elated when he took his final bow as LeFou that night. Scores of people left the auditorium cheerful and lighthearted because of him. (Some even left with an unexpected autograph!) In the beaming faces of the audience members cheering for Chris, I could readily see how willingness to receive accolades from others can spread joy.

Eager to learn more about this concept of sharing happiness which Chris seemed to instinctively understand, I needed to question the way I was raised to value societal etiquette and politeness more than the enrollment of others into my life. I had previously downplayed or cloaked my strengths and successes because I thought others might feel bad about themselves in comparison. I hadn't considered the notion that my politeness also repressed an opportunity for others to share in my joy. Comparison and worrying about what other people think blocks rather than fosters deep emotional attachments and I erred in thinking that others would choose comparison and judgment. Rather, I should believe in the generosity of others, such as those wonderful audience members at Chris' play.

This mindset of esteeming the accomplishments of others is rooted in honoring others' differences rather than comparing. It unifies and lifts others. Becoming enrolled in other's lives not only increases our happiness by sharing the happiness of others, but it can trigger something inside each of us to know we deserve the same.

With this new clarity about having confidence in diverse and different talents, I wanted to be more like Chris, who intuitively understood the Hollywood maxim that "there are no small parts." Recalling the various roles I'd played over my lifetime I could see episodes when I failed to act as the star of my own show. Quite the opposite from LeFou stealing the show, the way I acted in family, work and community parts sometimes made me look more like a side kick than the lead.

Believing I hadn't been or done enough also contributed to why I didn't flaunt my successes or expect accolades. Instead, I quickly debriefed my performance and focused ahead on the next goal. Thus, by constantly obscuring personal accomplishments I created my own false reality. Recalling my earlier judgment that Chris existed in a reality gap, I was humbled by the epiphany of it being more my issue than his.

No doubt, we each have accomplishments or have overcome hurdles deserving of applause. For me, raising children, adopting children (and feeding and clothing all of them), graduating from law school, winning cases, winning a local election and sitting as the School Board President—had all been cameo appearances in my life which I rarely touted. The more I thought about it, the clearer it became; by obscuring my successes I had been overcompensating to hide my secret pride. My reluctance to let Chris "show off" by labeling his confidence as false pride, was rooted in my judgement. I had been the one— not Chris—with the dysfunctional relationship between judgment and pride and I was anxious to let it go.

Although Professor Higgins hilariously portrayed a fool on stage, he was quite the opposite of LeFou in real life. His fearless belief in his stardom taught me how exhilarating life can be when I genuinely believe that *I am the star of my own show*—no matter the role—and that I can be happier when enrolling others into my life to support me. Truth is, we're each entitled to be the star of our own show.

I am taking my bows.

LESSON 15
Recognizing Superheroes Among Us

Except for some of the guys who dated his younger sisters, Chris loves others freely without reservation or judgment. He's an uninhibited, friendly guy who genuinely enjoys people. In high school he thought everyone was his friend. While walking across his high school campus, he offered and received dozens of "heys" and high-fives. Apparently, everyone *was* his friend.

When he was a young child, Chris' uninhibited friendliness toward strangers caused me great concern at stores, theaters, and especially in transient places like gas stations and parks. Many encounters served up interesting moments, and some were nerve-racking. Eventually I recognized how Chris' seemingly random selection of strangers provided life-altering lessons.

When Chris gave a thumbs up or called out to a stranger, "hey dude," or "yor cool," I looked up, expecting to greet a friend. But rarely was it someone we knew. I didn't always know what to say to these people who often looked as uncomfortable as I felt. A few would look away and pretend not to hear or see Chris, however most of the time people responded with a kind smile. Still, I was uneasy, and my nerves jumped every time he reached out to a stranger.

It was common to worry about the safety of young children in 1990s southern California. And because Chris' speech was difficult to understand, he was especially vulnerable. Struggling to know what to teach him about interacting with those we didn't know, I coached him about "stranger danger" but also about loving one another. I often pondered the wide contradictory spectrum between the two concepts but didn't quite know how to reconcile them. Always cognizant of the potential danger of kidnappings, it seemed critical for me to set boundaries to protect him and his younger sisters. Nonetheless, Chris would readily take candy from strangers! What was I to do?

This contradiction prompted me to examine my judgment of others. I noticed how I didn't mind as much when Chris spoke to a well-dressed person—especially dressed in a suit—but I was uneasy when he approached people with extensive tattoos and body piercings. In those days, people adorned this way seemed both exotic and dangerous; they looked the type to have criminal backgrounds. To give perspective, during the early 1990s, tattoos and body art weren't as mainstream as they are today and because I worked in the judicial system, I could recognize prison tattoos. The 1990s also ushered in an era of increased fear in Southern California. Brazen crimes against children headlined the news. Suburban kids no longer played unsupervised outside for hours or into the night and children were either sequestered inside their homes or escorted in public.

My uneasiness and worry turned to anxiety and distress the evening sixteen-year-old Chris and I attended his first World Wrestling Entertainment (WWE) event at the San Diego Sports Arena. Just being there made me uptight and uncomfortable. But when Chris exuberantly pounded the back of the heavily tatted guy seated next to him, I went into shock. While I calmed myself with breathing techniques, I learned years before in Lamaze class when pregnant, Chris looked thrilled as he gestured and yelled with his new friend. The young man had long, spiked blue hair and three chains dangling from three piercings on his nose linking to piercings on his right ear. It took all my energy to not stare, yet I still caught myself stealing glances of him out of the corner of my eye.

I longed to ask, "Doesn't that hurt? How do those chains not get tangled when you sleep or shower?" But I said nothing. Chris, however, didn't hesitate to talk with him—and didn't mention the chains.

I recalled the night of the dinner in our home about four years prior, when our local ward bishop was so accepting of Chris' WWE fetish. I'd come out of the closet and began my journey of accepting Chris' favorite sport. That night in the sports arena, however, was a new stretch of acceptance for me. I fought back my judgmental instincts, and sunk low in my chair, feeling awkwardly out of place.

Not long after the wrestling mayhem on stage began, Chris and his friend were sharing high-fives, cheering their favorite champions and booing the bad guys in unison. Rarely had I seen Chris so animated or happily engaged. I sat quietly on the other side of him enjoying the show! It wasn't the wrestling which entertained me, it was Chris' excitement and noticing the shift of my attitude toward the guy with the chains. It felt great to share a genuine smile as we said goodbye to the young man at the end of the evening. As I thanked him for making the event much more fun for my son, I gently touched his arm and sincerely wished him well in his life.

Another encounter with a stranger which I will never forget happened at Walmart™ when Chris was about seventeen. Walmart was usually my last choice of shopping sites, but Chris loved the store since they stocked WWE memorabilia. Chris wandered away from me while I looked at books. From an aisle away, I heard Chris exclaim, "Cool!" which, although loud, didn't alarm me. I just figured he found something he wanted to buy. But I jerked my head up when I heard a deep, booming male voice ask, "What? You talking to me?" The ominous voice came from the same proximity as where I thought Chris was, so I rushed my cart around the endcap to find my son. I panicked when I saw him at the other end of the aisle looking up at an exceptionally large—both tall and wide—man with a belly to match. A black leather vest hung from his shoulders exposing his beefy arms covered with black and gray tattoos—which looked like prison tats decorating almost every inch of the man's bare skin, including his bald head and neck. Everything about him was intimidating, even his heavy black boots with thick silver chains. Chris stood with his back to me, facing this man who was leaning against a shelf and studying my son. I had no doubt the man was a seasoned gang member.

I was so nervous that I almost tripped over my own feet as I hurried toward them. Before I could reach Chris, I saw him give the man a thumbs up while patting his own extended tummy as he repeated, "Cool!"

I felt light-headed, but a rush of adrenaline helped me quickly get to my son's side. Typically, whenever Chris approached people who made me nervous, I would try to graciously offer some type of apology while pulling Chris away. This time however, I feared the man—who Chris appeared to be mocking for his wide girth—probably had a brotherhood of men hanging out nearby. I must've been physically shaking as I blurted out, "Oh, my son appears to be impressed by your stature. Please excuse us." (*Stature?* I blushed at my word choice.) I met the man's eyes only for a second before looking at Chris and yanking his arm toward me to leave. But his feet were planted securely, and he refused to budge.

"Yor cool," Chris said. He gave the man a full-faced grin with clear admiration in his sparkling eyes. This drove my panic into high gear. I wondered how to explain to this gang member Chris's pure nature and how he wouldn't intentionally taunt him. Rather, Chris genuinely admired him. I had no idea how to make a smooth escape but knew we needed to. Immediately.

I stood wide-eyed and frozen beside my son as the man looked Chris up and down. After what seemed to be a long minute of silence but probably lasted only a few seconds, the man nodded slightly and said, "You look like you've eaten a horse or two yourself."

"Yuuup," Chris replied with a nod.

"What's your name, Buddy?" The man's face hinted at a slight smile.

I glanced at Chris as he turned to look at me. He didn't say anything, but I knew what his look meant. I gulped, hoping my fear wasn't too noticeable, and looked up, and up and up at the man. I translated Chris' thoughts in the most polite voice I could muster, with a feigned smile, "My son is probably wondering how you know Buddy is his nickname."

"That's because you're a cool dude and it *should* be your nickname." The man gave an even bigger smile as he cocked his head and looked directly at Chris. "What are you buying today?"

"Moovie," Chris reached into our cart, pulled out the

movie *Sharknado* and held it up with a proud grin.

I cringed with embarrassment. *Oh great,* I thought. *Now, if there's a scene and I have to call Security, everyone would know I buy ridiculous, brain-dead movies like Sharknado.* What sort of woman would buy that movie? (The obvious answer is: a woman who gets in precarious scenarios with dangerous men!)

"Oh, good choice, Buddy!" The man took the movie from Chris and eyed its cover.

Chris gave the man another thumbs up and mumbled words which I couldn't understand. I assumed he explained the theatrical value of a movie about a tornado intense enough to suck up sharks from the ocean and hurl them miles away.

"I know. It's a great movie," the man said as he re-placed it back in our cart.

That was the moment I melted. This man seemed to understand what Chris said even when I couldn't. Only a few people can clearly decipher Chris' mumbled speech. I stood silently while Chris and this man talked about other movies they liked. The man focused squarely on Chris' face, carefully listening before replying. The sincere interest and respect he showed for my son touched my heart. During the five to eight minutes we stood talking in the store aisle, both my prejudice and my guard thawed, and I felt a genuine smile form on my face. At the end of the conversation, I thanked him for his kindness in sharing his time with my son.

"Oh, not a problem," he replied. "You're a lucky mom."

"Yes, I really am. How amazing are you—not everyone understands that!" I gave an involuntary wink and a thumbs up and walked away holding Chris' hand. Chris turned to wave good-bye to our new friend and yelled with a confident nod, "Stay Cool!"

"You too, Buddy!" our new friend yelled back. We had made an unlikely friendship—and I grinned in disbelief as I realized I had just winked at a gang member. A nervous laugh escaped me, but I wondered if our alliance might come in handy someday if I ever needed protection.

Throughout his life Professor Higgins has taught me about the native goodness of people. We've shared many more educational encounters like the WWE event and the Walmart meeting which taught me to look for and see the good in people. I've been transforming from a mother who reminds her son not to talk to strangers to a fascinated participant in unexpected encounters. I no longer look at those I don't know through filters of judgment or fear and believe the strangers Chris chooses to interact with are not just random. I've learned to trust Chris' ability to see past people's outward appearance and into their hearts.

These days when Chris speaks to strangers, I smile and nod or exchange polite greetings, confident I have the pleasure of being in the presence of someone wonderful. Sometimes I stop and interpret Chris' messages for them, or I engage in a conversation curious to meet the person Chris has singled out. I'm no longer embarrassed when Chris reaches out to strangers, and I don't worry about their reactions. Now, I smile and remain awestruck by the continual flow of new acquaintances and friends into our lives. I haven't forgotten the days before having the privilege of loving a child with Down syndrome when I would've judged people who looked different.

Chris' siblings and I value his superpower to read hearts and often jest about his usefulness as a "human litmus test" for detecting people with good souls. On occasion his sisters have secretly tested their crushes by introducing them to Chris to note his reaction. If Chris likes the new friend, it helps his sisters decide if they will continue to date. Although he loves others easily, he warms up more to some—who are good-hearted—than others. And I'm often pleased to see how some people naturally know how to connect with Chris and receive his love. They somehow know how to not baby him or talk down to him, but they simply accept Chris as he is and see his genuine worth. This acceptance alone elicits my acceptance and respect for them.

Chris hasn't gone unrewarded for his superpower of attracting beautiful people. For example, one Christmas when Chris was thirty, I found about fifteen different gift cards in his wallet.

"Where did you get all these gift cards?" I asked.

"Friends a da gym," he replied in his usual matter-of-fact tone.

"Which friends? In exchange for what?" Chris worked out at the gym three times a week with his Care-Rite job coach in the mornings while I was at work. I worried because we didn't have any family friends who mentioned they saw Chris at the gym.

"What are your friend's names?" I probed further.

"Umhhh." And with a shrug of his shoulders, he had nothing else to say about it.

"My Buddy, you have over $150 in gift cards, and you don't know their names?" I asked.

He replied with a cheeky, "Hee Hee."

I later asked his job coach about the gift cards, and she explained there were lots of kind men at the gym who routinely encouraged Chris on the treadmill. They talked every week, and some matched their schedules to be there at the same time to cheer him on. Those generous gifts were repeated every Christmas for as long as he attended the gym. I've never met those men, but it has melted my heart knowing there are heroes in the world who show such kindness to my son—especially when I'm not around to interpret for him or protect him.

Chris has special attachments to many people and has adopted some friends as family by calling them brothers, cousins, aunts and uncles. He means it. It's a love title for life.

He refers to my sister (his Aunt KayLani) as Aunt Mae, Spiderman's kind, loving aunt. Everyone else sees a strong, determined, smart woman who is a force of nature, but Chris sees KayLani as kind and loving. Since Chris can't write text messages, KayLani sends him pictures and memes. No matter how busy she is with her own 6 children and 13 grandchildren, for years she has carved out time to send hundreds of text pictures.

"Aww," I heard Aunt KayLani sigh when Chris called her Aunt Mae, "Thank you for seeing the good in me."

Chris called Herb, my late brother, "Superman." Although I always knew my brother to be a compassionate and exceptionally nice man, I originally thought Chris' choice of nickname to be a bit off. Herb had many strengths: he was brilliant, inventive, accomplished, generous, funny and kind. Although he loved wilderness adventures, I wouldn't describe him as the strong, powerful character typical of Superman. However, when his Uncle Herb lived with us in his later years, I saw Chris' joyful interactions with him and realized I had never truly known my brother. I delighted seeing Herb through Chris' eyes; they played tag around the house and even if Herb was working, he never seemed bothered when Chris interrupted him with a startling, "Tag yor it!" They played daily and for thirty-forty minutes—which I considered to be irritatingly prolonged periods of time. But my brother laughed and surprised Chris right back.

Although I was in my fifties, I came to know my brother better, and also came to know Chris better as I overheard their long conversations about sports, friends, and TV shows. Herb was a real friend to his nephew; he noticed when Chris appeared upset and cared enough to know why. One day Herb explained to me why Chris became angry every time I moved his WWE figures when dusting his bedroom. Chris was thirty years old at the time and had been collecting figures since he was eight. He had hundreds of WWE figures, stacked ten deep on bookshelves all around his room, and it took a long time to remove and replace all the figures during cleaning. Herb explained how Chris had intentionally organized them by differing championship titles, rivalries and winners. I never imagined there to be a sophisticated organizational arrangement for what I thought were merely toys. I had no idea Chris was that clever! After learning this, I changed my cleaning protocol to keep the figures in their exact order and enjoyed Chris' grateful smile and hug each time I finished dusting. (Thank you, Superman.)

Uncle Herb died in 2017. To this day, whenever Chris and I pass the local hospital Herb stayed in for extended medical treatment, Chris blows a kiss toward the hospital and says, "Superman's hosbital." And I think to myself, "Wow! I'm so lucky to have been Superman's sister."

However, my greatest blessing has been to have a son who could introduce me to Superman, and to so many other superheroes in the world.

LESSON 16

Liberation From Fantasy Fears

C hris loves to go to the movies. Although I am his loyal escort to the theater, we do *not* see chick flicks or romance comedies which I'd enjoy. Instead, I martyr up and take Chris to see all the adventure filled, horrifying, sci-fi, thrilling, superhero movies I can tolerate—and then some. Cue the Wolverine.

One night, however, I got way more than I bargained for from the price of show tickets. Who knew watching *The Mummy* could be a transformational movie date I'd never forget? When the story plot included a visit to the City of the Dead, I should have been more prepared for the inevitable ghastly sights. I sat frozen in horror with both hands clenching the arms of my seat during the scene of a Scarab attack with thousands of flesh eating beetles. After being startled by the sound of my own shriek of terror, I sank back into my seat with embarrassment.

Chris gently put his hand over mine, leaned in close and whispered, "Mom, it's not weal."

His peaceful demeanor snapped me back to reality. I inhaled slowly, grateful for the wave of calmness which passed through me and then laughed sheepishly over the irony of Chris having a better grasp on reality than I had.

It was both embarrassing and hysterical to me that my twenty-three year-old son who believed in Santa, Vulcans, wizarding, and that Elvis is still alive, could so readily disengage from a movie scene. Considering that Hollywood's brilliant artistry is designed purposely to invoke pseudo emotions and transport the audience into a fantasy world, how was Chris so unaffected? And why was I much more easily influenced by the theater's magic? Whatever the reason, Chris showed no fear and simply appreciated the adventure.

After I regained control over my imagination and reminded myself that I was simply watching a fictional movie, I was able to relax, sit back with Chris and our imaginary new friend, Brendan Fraser, and just enjoyed the show.

I later thought about this irony many times. When finding myself anxiously worrying about my family and fearful of the future, Chris' advice of "Mom, it's not weal," echoed in my mind. Why did I worry so often and about so many things? I recalled the many concerns I had carried throughout my son's life which had been based on beliefs and information which turned out to be incorrect. Eventually I discovered that many of those issues turned out to be merely fantasies I had made up. My life could have been more peaceful and calmer if I had been able to discern which worries were reasonable to carry with me and which I should give up.

Perhaps part of my problem was that I had grown accustomed to worrying. It had been one of my closest companions throughout my life. (I had to ask myself if maybe it had become a bad habit I simply needed to break.) Since Chris' birth, I had allowed fears over every aspect of his life to consume me, such as what will happen to him if I die and who would take care of him? Will he be sickly and how long will he live? Will he be able to talk, communicate his basic needs, and have autonomy over his life? Will he be capable of sharing an emotional bond with his siblings, know joy and happiness, be smart and accomplished enough? Will have friends or suffer a life without love (other than from family)? Will people make fun of him or bully him, and would he be the last kid picked for a team, or even be allowed to participate in group sports?

It was as if I were standing on a slippery slope of fears when Chris was very young, and I had no factual basis for what my son's future would look like. Essentially, I worried about everything because I wasn't sure about anything—from my initial concerns over the effect of a Down syndrome diagnosis to fearing the many assumed hardships my son and our entire family would inevitably face. (I had no idea what the hardships would be, only that they should be expected and would probably bring sorrow or misery.)

Fear of the unknown is one of the most pernicious worries because of its inability to be resolved.

The cruelest fear I've ever faced was based on my doctor's initial prediction that Chris wouldn't live past the age of seven. I had naively celebrated the year following his seventh birthday and just figured that my son was lucky to have beaten the odds—that he was living on borrowed time. It wasn't until Chris turned nine that I realized there'd never been a real basis to justify my belief in the doctor's opinion. Other than having a weakened immune system which made him slow to heal from routine viruses and resulting in serious respiratory illnesses, Chris had been relatively healthy.

That perceived, but false reality was unrealistic and based on unenlightened medical advice, common throughout centuries of medical experience. Upon realizing this, I mourned not only the needless energy and time I spent worrying, but also the loss of opportunities for joy.

The seven year battle between my inner advice to protect my heart from the inevitable pain of Chris' early death had taken a toll on me and my marriage. But in losing the battle, I had accepted how fully in love and attached I was to my beautiful little boy.

All that pent up pain from preparing to lose him early in his life made me angry over my false beliefs and fueled my resolution to never again rely solely on professionals' opinions about my son's future. But anxiety about the uncertainties in Chris' life remained buried in me.

I wondered how much happier and peaceful my life would've been if I were able to identify which fears were based on my imagination and were without facts.

Wouldn't it be nice if I had someone constantly looking over my shoulder when I'm afraid and whispering, "it's not weal," when appropriate? It would require a brilliant seer to do that. However, Chris seemed up to the task.

What did Chris know that I didn't? How had Hollywood's magic not sucked him away from remaining in the present? The question itself held the answer. The key to mastering fears of the future begins with the ability to genuinely embrace the present—one of Chris' superpowers. He rarely spent time worrying or thinking about the future. He always has and still lives in the now. When he's watching a movie, he's not in the movie. He's either in a theatre or his house—enjoying the entertainment.

This was how Professor Higgins showed me how to take charge of my imagination and fears. To do this I needed to be able to filter which of my worries were grounded in the present—or reality—and which were linked to my imagination (or someone else's).

Fantasy fears, based on assumptions or imagination about the unknown, were the most pernicious and debilitating to me in my past. Those were the worries which looped in my head and were never resolved.

Eventually I found one straightforward way to process each worry by using a sort of fact (reality) or fantasy triage. This sorting process readily illuminated fears I had about Chris's life that were based purely on imaginary problems or were fantastical expectations about the unknown.

Because real solutions cannot be applied to illusory problems, being unable to formulate a resolution was another way to determine that my worries were unsupported by facts and based on fantasy. Using this analysis, the decision of which fears to abandon became as obvious as finding scorpions in the desert night.

By staying grounded in the present, my fears surrounding Chris seemed to dissipate. I no longer worried about Chris not having friends or not being accepted. He has had so many friends—Tara's friends, school friends, church friends, Boy Scout friends, Care-Rite friends, even nameless friends at the gym.

I no longer worried that people will tease or bully Chris or treat him as an outcast because I'd never seen it happen to him. To determine whether a fear is based on reality, I found that I simply needed to find facts to support it. For example, I assessed my fear of what will happen to Chris if I die and who would take care of him. It is undisputed that I will, in fact, die one day, therefore, my worries for his care in the future were based in reality and should be addressed. This legitimate fear propelled me to create an estate plan.

As I made financial plans and nominated who would

care for Chris, my worries lessened. It was such a relief and comfort to hear his siblings, family members and even friends offer to become Chris' guardian. My heart smiled hearing everyone lightheartedly wrestle over which of them would support his passion for WWE, his disdain for hiking and his love of whoopie cushions. My fears were resolved and replaced with joy and peace.

Finding reliable facts can be difficult in unexpected situations. And because there has been insufficient historical information about genetic conditions, including Trisomy 21, determining between facts and assumptions hasn't always been easy. Other parents in the Down syndrome community have consistently been among my best resources to determine truth. Their factual feedback about their children has helped me identify if any of my concerns are based in reality or myths. Collaborating with these parents also brings many moments of laughter as we share information regarding the similarities, uniqueness, and the *downright* charming idiosyncrasies of our children.

Looking at my son's future without unjustified fears has increased my delight with his life. I'm free from worrying over issues without articulable solutions or supporting facts. This freedom has allowed me to relax, sit back with Chris and "enjoy the show" of our lives. It has even given me the courage to tackle bigger problems—such as some which could be tantamount to facing an army of mummies alongside Brandon Fraiser.

Wait. Stop. That's "not weal."

DOCTORATE COURSES

LESSON 17

On Being A Man

"**I** no like Down syndrome," Chris proclaimed as I walked into the family room where he was watching TV.

His words sucker punched me. "What?" I stopped short and stared at him.

"I no like Down syndrome." He shook his head back and forth.

I stood frozen for a moment until it hit me that he must've overheard the phone conversation I just had with his doctor's office. I replayed the tape back in my mind of what I said that could've triggered this reaction. I know I mentioned his medical diagnosis to explain that although he was in his twenties, I was speaking on his behalf, but nothing else. I was bewildered.

I sat down on the couch to process his announcement and hopefully understand it.

"My Buddy, will you sit with me for a minute?" I patted a spot on the couch next to me. As he walked over, I noticed his creased brow and the serious look in his eyes.

"What is there not to like about Down syndrome?" I asked gently. "I love it!"

He looked away and shrugged his shoulders.

"Do you think having Down syndrome could somehow be bad?" I put my hand on his cheek.

Chris pulled his face away and slowly nodded. I was dumbfounded.

"But I think Down syndrome is wonderful! It means I'm one of the luckiest moms in the world—because of you." I grabbed his shoulders and turned him toward me. Looking closely into his beautiful round eyes, I searched his facial expression for any clue to figure out why he would say such a thing. I hoped it was merely a fleeting notion, but based on the downcast look on his face, I knew he was serious and genuinely sad.

"My Buddy, please tell me what I don't know," I begged.

Chris shrugged. I waited. We looked at each other in silence for several long moments. I could tell he was counting on me to read his mind. I couldn't. I was horrified and willing to wait as long as it took for him to explain.

He finally broke the silence by slowly saying, "Eh means netarded. I no like netarded."

His words speared my heart and knocked me back into the couch cushion. My hands spontaneously rushed to cover my chest to put pressure on my wounded heart.

What happened to him? Other than an incident when he was at a restaurant with Aubrey and me years earlier, I didn't know he'd heard the "R-word." I feared that someone had bullied or teased him, and I hadn't been there to protect him.

Thinking he wouldn't understand a technical medical diagnosis, I said, "Oh Buddy, you're not retarded! I'm not really sure what that word means, but you're smart and have so many talents and abilities."

Chris wasn't swayed. "Down syndrome may be in the cells of your body, but you decide what's in your heart and mind—that's who you are," I continued.

I paused for his reply, but he only blinked.

"You're so smart about singing, acting, and you even know things I don't know—like how to love."

He nodded. (Ouch!)

"It's not the same thing!" I insisted. "People with Down syndrome are superheroes who make the world a happy place—with your love…and how funny you are…and cute…and charming…and you're My Buddy." Soothing him with those words in a slightly melodic and hypnotic tone usually brought him around.

Not this time.

"Down syndrome is awesome! But if it makes you sad, I won't say it anymore. I'm sorry."

Chris gave me a thumbs up.

"Will that make you happy?"

He forced an exaggerated toothy smile which meant,

"yes." I sighed with relief but remained consumed with sorrow.

"But can I still call you my Downy Boy?"[3] I asked with a hint of desperation.

"Uuh Huh." He leaned in for a bear hug. Oh, how his hugs can heal my heart.

One of my favorite lullabies to sing to Chris when he was a young child was our personal version of an old traditional Irish ballad called, "Oh Danny Boy." Our own lyrics:

> *My Downy Boy, I'm glad, I'm glad you came to me, Sweet, full of love, oh please don't ever go.*
> *It's you and me, together we will always be, Now go to sleep, and know I love you so.*

Our song always triggered love—in both of us; it was only ours and we didn't even share it with his siblings. Our love song birthed Chris' first nickname when he was a baby, "My Downy Boy." As he grew older and his nickname changed to "My Buddy," I was slow to give up his first pet name, but occasionally when we enjoyed a private moment sitting together or when tucking him into bed at night, I'd lean in close to whisper, I love my

---

[3] I am sensitive to the potential of this term being offensive to some in the Down syndrome community, and I do not seek to offend. In the early 1980's I made up this private nickname—based on the real song, "Oh Danny Boy." I don't use it in public and am not suggesting it is appropriate for anyone else to use this term. I am only including this to explain Chris' journey in becoming a man.

Downey Boy"—and he'd melt into his sheets (especially when I added, "no Boy Scouts tomorrow").

Still holding Chris and gently rocking him as we sat on the couch, I began softly singing our song into his ear, *"My Downy Boy, I'm glad, I'm glad you came to me...,"* but the wound in my heart spread to my voice, cracking it. I stopped, not wanting him to know how sad I was to not be able to protect him from feeling less than the amazing person he was.

Yet again, I longed to convince the world to stop using the "R-word." If only I could yell loud enough for everyone to hear, "It's a medical term and should never be thoughtlessly used as a joke or epithet!"

I quickly wiped away my tears and leaned out of our hug. A normal smile had returned to his face, and all seemed well again. (One of his superpowers is how fast he forgives.)

I've never forgotten my dark discussion with Chris that day. Out of habit, but with his permission, I continued using his pet name on rare occasions—particularly when he was unhappy or mad, because it always soothed him and drew a smile.

But a few years later when he was in his mid-twenties, he made a second bold proclamation which rocked my world.

It was a chilly Saturday in February, when Chris and I were sitting together on the couch, quietly watching the fire. I still vividly recall everything about that afternoon. I had a few extra minutes before leaving to meet friends for dinner and was happy to have time to sit with My Buddy. His head laid on my shoulder while I gently scratched his neck and cheek. My mind was meandering when suddenly, he pulled his head away, sat up straight and turned to look me squarely in the eyes. He loudly cleared his throat and carefully said, "Mom, I not Downy Boy. I am Downy Man."

My eyes popped open as my chin fell. It was just so random! I don't know if I was more startled by his direct demeanor, his articulate declaration or what he said.

As the shock wore off, I figured his announcement meant he didn't want to be babied. How cute! (Oops…I caught and immediately squelched my instinctive mollycoddling reaction.)

"What do you mean by Downy Man?" I asked.

"Humh," he replied. He cuddled in next to me and looked back at the fire as if to say, "I'm glad we had this conversation." I waited for him to explain further. Apparently, he had nothing more to say on the subject.

Right or wrong, I knew I flagrantly and unapologetically doted over my precious son. And his sisters pampered him too (except when it came to housework). It was easy and fun to love him! Before the recent adoption of his cousins, Jared and Jason as his new brothers, we had been an all-female family who nurtured and adored Chris. And Chris seemed to bask in our loving care and never complained—until now. Was he outgrowing our adoration and care?

Jared has teased me and my daughters many times in the past over the way we "treated Chris like a puppy dog." His sisters and I snickered at the comparison while Aubrey reached over and gave Chris' cheek a little jiggle. In a baby voice she'd usually add, "We don't do that, do we Buddy?" Chris laughed along with everyone—except Jared who just shook his head back and forth. Many times he tried to convince me to stop babying Chris, but I just couldn't.

I assumed Chris' statement meant that he no longer wanted to be treated like a child. But what would being a man entail? As we cuddled silently by the fire, I felt a bit lost and confused. Because of the way he made the announcement—by clearing his throat—I knew I needed to listen to him, to somehow treat him differently and try to honor his request.

Perhaps it was time for a change. The thought that it could be the end of an era made me melancholy, and I worried I wasn't ready to let go of my forever child. He was a love bucket I could rely on—never to empty.

I finally broke our long silence. "Does this mean you aren't a boy anymore—and you're a man? I'm a little lost, Buddy."

"Eee Hee," he said somberly with a slow nod.

"Well, if that's how you feel I won't call you 'My Downy Boy' anymore. But I don't think I can call you Downy Man." Teasingly I added, "We might have to give up our song 'cuz 'Oh Downy Man' doesn't sound right. Are you ready for that?" (I only felt a little bad about my manipulative attempt to avoid this change—I'm still a work in progress.)

Chris nodded, stood up and went to his room leaving me not only surprised and bemused, but also impressed. My head spontaneously shook with worry as he walked away. What just happened? What does Chris' version of being a man look like? What would I need to do differently?

Later that night, while I was enjoying dinner with my friends, Chris called.

"Hey! What's up, My Buddy?"

"You come home? Tuck me in?" he asked.

"I'll be home pretty soon Buddy," I assured him. "Your sister can tuck you in."

"Come home...tuck me in," he whined.

I grinned. I loved tucking him into bed at night but couldn't resist teasing him. "My Buddy, remember, you want to be a man now? Men don't need to be tucked in." (My friends looked at me askew. Who has these types of unusual conversations?)

"Come hooome...tuck me iiiin." Chris moaned even louder.

"Buddy, I'm having a nice time with my friends. I promise to check on you when I get home, but if you want to go to bed now, ask one of your sisters to tuck you in."

I hung up, giggling—torn between enjoyment, confusion and relief over my son's short-lived request to be a man. Chris was our own real-life version of Prince Charming. Of course, I never wanted to stop tucking him in and singing him songs.

Upon arriving home, I went directly upstairs and found Chris lying flat on his back on the floor at the threshold of his bedroom door.

He whimpered, "Tuuuck meee iiin!"

I hadn't been away long enough to cause him any pain; it was only 9:30 pm on a Saturday night and he normally didn't go to bed until at least 11:00 pm. But Prince Charming had turned into a drama King!

Tara heard me come home and yelled assurances from her bedroom that she tried to tuck him in, but he refused her.

"Ok My Buddy, I'll tuck you in," I laughed. "But someday we need to talk seriously about what it might look like for you to become a man. And I'm pretty sure being tucked into bed will be on the chopping block."

"Uh-huh," Chris mumbled and rubbed his eyes. As I arranged his blanket snugly around his shoulders and arms I softly said, "I think you're going to like being a man, My Buddy." I tried to sound credible, but I didn't believe my own words.

Chris nodded and with palpable relief closed his eyes, snuggled under his covers and drifted off to sleep. All was well in his world again.

Over the next weeks and months, I frequently thought

about Chris expressing his desire to be a man. But the more I thought about it the more I worried—even panicked. I had no idea how to encourage him or whether I should. Would he want to live on his own? How could I take care of him and protect him if I lost control over everything in his world? I was hitting walls harboring my greatest fears for my son's future.

Hopefully, he didn't want more freedom and responsibility, but only wanted to be treated respectfully rather than being babied.

I could not be at peace until I figured it out.

Given Chris' developmental level, I worried he wouldn't be capable of being a man in the sense of taking on full responsibility to care for himself. But I knew of other people with Trisomy 21 who seemed impressively capable—some were married, one man raised a son who didn't have Down syndrome, another young woman had a driver's license.

Although I didn't know how things could shift, I accepted Chris's desire for change. And slowly, over the next few years, they did.

The first thing I noticed was how he used his voice more and asked for what he wanted. Hooray! Although this opened the door for more potential conflicts, it also brought unexpected and fun new experiences.

One day he showed me his wallet and pointed to the inside, filled only with gift cards.

"I nee-money." He rubbed the figures of one hand together.

"Why?" I asked. I always paid for everything—he never needed money.

"I like money."

I had no idea what he meant but gave him some cash, curious to see what could happen. The next time we went to the movies, he handed the cashier his money to pay for our tickets, gave her a wink and stepped away with a bit of a pep in his step.

I made a point to check his wallet as often as I could afford to restock his cash. He routinely offered to pay for meals or grocery store purchases when we were out together. I usually supplemented our purchase with a debit card, but Chris clearly enjoyed paying for me. And I was delighted to watch his confidence grow.

"Go to bank? Get my money?" he asked one day as he handed me his paycheck. He worked a few hours a week with a job coach through Care-Rite and I deposited his occasional paychecks into our joint bank account. I thought it was a great idea to show Chris how his paper paycheck turned into money. We drove to the bank, and I watched him proudly print his name on his check. He stood straighter than normal as he smiled and handed it to the banker with his ID.

I quietly mouthed, "All one dollar bills, please."

His eyes widened and his mouth gaped open as the teller slowly counted out $53.00 and pushed the large stack of bills directly in front of him.

Chris raised both arms—like a touchdown, and

boomed, "I'm filthy rich!" I noticed several people all around the bank turn to stare at us as I pulled his arms lower.

"What are you going to do with all your money?" The teller grinned at Chris.

"Buy mom hat and new car," Chris confidently declared. His words warmed my heart and turned my cheeks red. He stuffed the wad of bills in his wallet, turned and walked with me out of the bank, as if he were walking on a red carpet—the picture of success. And I was sure he looked a little taller as he held the door open for me. His generous care for me felt wonderful. Hysterical, but nonetheless wonderful. (I didn't need a hat but would've loved a new car!)

Chris' desire to provide and take care of me became more apparent as time moved on. One day he broke his foot but refused to stay home from Care-Rite claiming, he "needed to go to work to make money." But he came home distressed that afternoon—not due to any pain, but because Care-Rite wouldn't let him return without clearance from a doctor. Chris was depressed for weeks over missing work until the day finally came for the doctor to remove his protective boot. After the doctor carefully assessed Chris' foot, he announced that it would be a couple more weeks before Chris could walk without support.

Chris threw his hands in the air and yelled, "Doctor, I have da work...pay the rent!" The look of exasperation on his face was as real as it gets.

The doctor jerked his head around and glared at me, alarmed I would force my son to work and support me. I placed my palm on my forehead as my head shook, "no."

"Don't worry Chris, we're fine." I was embarrassed, but grateful when the doctor appeared relieved by my assurance. (You can bet we talked more about his misunderstanding of our family finances on the way home.)

A few months later during dinner one night, Aubrey asked if we'd noticed lately how Chris happened to always be the first to open the front door when Kathryn or Tara expected a date to arrive. I recalled noticing him sitting closer to his bedroom door with it wide open so he could hear the doorbell over his TV. We laughed as we realized his dash to open the door and be the first to greet their dates, was not a coincidence, but calculated.

Chris welcomed the young men he liked—eagerly. But he coldly scrutinized those he didn't know. On occasion, he eyed their date and sternly said, "Take care of ma sista."

"What?" one young man asked Kathryn.

"Oh, he just said, "have fun with my sister." She quickly stepped out the front door.

We were usually charmed by Chris' protective care, but one day we were shocked and embarrassed when he opened the door to Kathryn's new suitor and said, "Humph!" and slammed the door closed in his face.

"Why'd you do that?" Kathryn demanded as she ran to the door and yanked it open.

"Not Cody." Chris growled. Apparently, he wasn't happy Kathryn had broken up with Cody and was dating someone new. (Another one of Chris' superpowers was his unerring discerning assessment of true character, and he had been a loyal ally to a few of his sister's close friends.)

Chris' new protective behaviors expanded dramatically when he asked for his own NCIS badge for Christmas. I thought he simply wanted a Hollywood prop for play acting, but armed with this badge, Chris took on a new persona. Every time Chris knew we would go through a security check point (especially at the airport) he brought his badge to show the officers. (He still does this with a confident "thumbs up.") Some officers have been cool and smiled or nodded to Chris with respect while others simply gawked at us with uncertainty. (I secretly giggled with pride over having my own pseudo private security escort.)

One day, however, Chris went a little too far. I didn't personally witness it all, but learned about it from our good friend, Richard LaPort. Upon arriving home from work one evening, I saw Richard drive up with his daughter, Laura, and Chris in his car. Richard had generously offered to drive Chris home from play practice because I had worked too late. As soon as Richard saw me, he jumped out of his car and ran toward me, laughing.

"I...I...I have to tell you what happened." He could

barely speak through his laughter. "It was...seriously... the funniest thing I've...ever seen." He wiped away laughter tears from his eyes.

I giggled with anticipation as I watched him struggle to compose himself. He took a deep breath and haltingly described his arrival to pick up Chris and Laura from the local senior center.

"I saw Chris sitting on the bench outside by the front door waiting for me." He covered his mouth to stop another chortle. "I had just stepped out of my car but froze when two police vehicles pulled up to the en-trance—lights flashing and sirens wailing—something was happening. The first officer jumped out of his patrol car and ran to the door *with his gun drawn*. Suddenly, Chris stood up in front of the officer, put his hand up to stop the officer and flashed some sort of badge at him. Chris yelled, 'It's OK. I got this.'" Richard doubled over in laughter.

My hand quickly caught my forehead as it dropped. "Ahhh!" I wasn't laughing...or breathing. I had been a police dispatcher while in college and knew the serious-ness of a Code Three emergency police response.

I stared in disbelief as Richard continued, "the officer stopped in front of Chris, quickly sized him up, shook his head and ran around him into the building." Richard burst into laughter again and gasped for air. "It was like watching a slapstick comedy unfold in real life."

"It was probably his NCIS badge," I interrupted. "Oh

my! Chris could've been shot!"

Richard noticed my frozen smile and drew in a deep breath to compose himself. "I know! Everyone was safe — it was a false alarm. But, what a great police officer!"

"I agree." I added breathlessly, "I'm so thankful for fast thinking officers!"

Richard's earnestness quickly ebbed as he added, "I'm sorry, I just can't stop laughing, but nothing bad happened."

All the oxygen I didn't know I was holding in finally rushed out as I relaxed enough to enjoy the story.

"You should've seen the look on Chris's face! It was so surreal...and when he said, 'I've got this'—so clearly and with authority." We both enjoyed another round of laughter at the incredulous story.

"Whew! We dodged that bullet—literally!" I grinned with my pun, said goodbye and thanked Richard for bringing Chris home safely.

Later that night when tucking Chris into bed I asked, "What happened at the Senior Center today?" I tried to sound calm, but inside I was still a bit nervous.

"Cops." He said.

"What did you do?"

"Helped....securdy."

"Were you protecting your friends?" I asked.

"Yuuup." He confidently replied.

I smiled and we locked eyes for a moment. "Your friends are safe with you. That was very brave. Do you like protecting people?"

"Yuuup."

"That's what good men do." Chris nodded his agreement.

"But, Buddy, if you see police officers again—especially when their cars have flashing lights, or you hear sirens—you can stand down and wait for them to tell you how to help."

"Eee-hee," he replied.

"I was a police dispatcher when you were a little boy. They taught me that if there are bad guys around, the officers will want to handle everything. But they can let you know what help they need. And you can help a lot by sitting down and staying safely out of the way."

"Eee-hee," he repeated.

"So, what would you do if you see a police officer with a gun again, or lights on his car, or if you can hear a siren?

Chris sang his reply, "Bad boys, bad boys whatcha gonna do. Whatcha gonna do when day come for you?"

"Exactly. I'm glad we had this deeply meaningful talk." I smiled. (And that was as successful as some of our conversations often were.)

Even though many years have passed since Chris stopped the approaching police officer, Richard and I still laugh whenever we talk about our memory of Chris' brave desire to protect everyone in the Senior Center.

Although Chris lives in an alternate reality, his quest to become his own man remains his universal right and privilege. It began with his protesting being labeled. His intuitive understanding that a diagnosis of Down syndrome did not define him and was merely one aspect of his multi-faceted persona, was right on. Standing for something he believed in opened the door to growth and change—for everyone in our family, not just him. His progression into manhood was manifested by voicing his need to abandon his childhood pet name, to insist on not being babied and to go after what he wanted.

I don't hold myself out to be an expert on understanding what it takes to be a man. But because I trust Professor Higgins' innate knowledge, I have pondered the lessons I could take from watching the changes in him.

Based on Chris' teachings, I believe there are at least two foundational traits at the heart of a real man. First, a man desires to take a stand on matters important to him or which pertain to his own life. Secondly, a man wants to protect and provide for those he cares about—not because others are less capable—but because it fulfills him and is his way of showing love. I now believe that inside every real man is an innate desire and ability to be a true hero.

With this understanding, I shifted my perspective and appreciation for my father's overprotective nature—which I used to resent and push against. I realized his overbearing and often micro-managing advice wasn't as much about control as it was about valor and love. Luckily, Professor Higgins offered me this lesson before my father died, allowing me time to honor him during his later years as my hero and to thank him for his protection and zeal in providing for my mother, my siblings and me.

Although my respect for Chris' desire to live a man's life hasn't subsided, I constantly must check my compulsive desire to coddle him. Recently, when tucking Chris into bed, we playfully argued over what song I should sing.

"I miss our old song, "Oh Downy Boy," I teased. "But of course, I can't sing it since you're a man now." My voice hinted of both teasing and wistfulness over missing my baby boy.

"Eee-hee." Chris nodded with an air of dignity.

"We need a new song. What's a man's song?" I asked.

"Danny Manny." His serious look quickly broke into an impish grin and his whole body jiggled with laughter.

I shook my head. "No, I'll do corny, but not crazy." Then I laughed and jiggled right back.

We never came up with a new song and just let the old song go...peacefully into our past.

On his terms and in his own way, Chris became the man in our family—even a hero. But he has never stopped asking me to tuck him in, sing him a song and kiss him goodnight. Why not?

Manhood is a wonderful thing.

LESSON 18
Being Loyal To Santa

S anta Claus has always been one of Chris' life-long champions, right up there with superheroes like Captain America and Ironman. Their only, but significant, difference is that Chris knows Captain America and Ironman exist only in the Marvel Universe and are not part of our world.

Not only is Santa real to Chris, but he is also Chris' real kind of hero. Why wouldn't he be? Delightful festivities and Christmas music abound as the world celebrates Santa's annual appearance. And to top it all off, hot chocolate flows in abundance and cookies are too numerous to be counted until Christmas day.

Chris and Chris Kringle are kindred spirits; they love everyone and see the good in people. More than simply being nice, Santa is heroic because he cares enough about each child individually to know their names, addresses and which special gift will fulfill every heart's desire. Chris and Santa are unified in their desire for everyone to be happy. Neither Chris' loyalty nor his faith in the miracles of Christmas have ever waned. Because of Chris, I've remained loyal to Santa well beyond those magical years when my children were young. I hung in there through Chris' teenage years when his list for Santa included challenging gifts such as the Excalibur Sword or Harry Potter's invisibility cloak. But as the years passed, I became covertly resentful over my forever child's endless quest for magic. Would there ever be a final Claus for Santa?

When Chris was about twenty-six years old, the fateful day finally came when I decided to have "the talk" with him about the true nature of his beloved St. Nicholas. As soon as I set up the Christmas tree, Chris handed me a picture cut from his WWE magazine of his current favorite wrestler, John Cena.

"Presents! Eee-Hee!" Chris' entire body shimmied with excitement.

"But you already have a John Cena figure," I said, puzzled.

"Belt." Chris pointed to the large, gold Championship Title Belt around John Cena's waist and bobbed his head with an expectant look of sheer joy.

"Um…sorry, but a belt like that costs hundreds of dollars and I can't afford a gift like…"

"Santa Claus," Chris interrupted. I forced myself to look away from the happiness beaming through his huge smile and eager nods.

"Santa could never afford a gold belt either." I assured him.

"Santa can." Chris had no doubt.

"Santa's elves can't make a gold wrestling belt!" I asserted, but Chris simply shrugged his shoulders.

"WWE Championship Belts can't be given as gifts; they can only be won!" I sputtered out my best argument.

"Santa can." Chris left the room, his faith in Santa undaunted.

I took a deep breath. Chris' list for Santa had grown more unrealistic each year. I knew it would be foolish to waste hundreds of dollars on a gold belt he would never wear—especially at Christmastime when there are many better ways to spend money and help others. Since Chris would probably never move out of my house, would my Santa budget continue to rise with Chris' age? I sighed and felt my Jolly Meter diving into Scrooge territory, indicating the time for the big reveal about Santa had come. My budget couldn't handle the two of us; Santa had to go.

I walked into Chris' room, sat down on his bed and invited him to sit next to me. "Chris, I need to tell you something very important. Santa Claus isn't real. The Santa you see each year at parties wears a costume, like on Halloween. The stories about Santa are not true—they are only stories made up for little children. And you aren't little anymore."

"Huh?" Chris's look of surprise quickly turned to confusion.

I took his hands in mine. "Santa is not real, Bud. He's pretend—just like Captain America."

Chris squinted at me and said nothing.

"I'm sorry for the bad news, but you need to know the truth." I bit my lip. I didn't want to hurt him.

Chris' squint turned to a glare as he jerked his hands out of mine. "You a liar! Santa *is* weal!" His disgust and rage sharpened his speech and surprised me. I'd never seen Chris so angry. He jumped up and assumed a battle stance with his hands fisted by his sides.

"Liar!" Chris glared directly into my eyes with a clear intent to defend Santa's honor.

"Well...technically, you're right and I'm very sorry." I responded as tenderly as possible. I had to admit Chris had a point—essentially, I had been lying to him his entire life. It was true; I was a liar.

"Take eh back!" Chris ordered through clenched teeth while still frozen in battle stance.

"I can't, My Buddy." I grimaced, feeling Chris' pain. "You're old enough to know the truth. All those gifts from Santa? Well, I bought them for you. And all the stories about Santa are just made up. He's not real."

"He *is* weal. You ah wong...an mean!"

I loudly exhaled. I didn't know what to say; my apology and explanations only seemed to make the disclosure worse. I offered a feeble excuse about needing to do something and walked out of his room, just ahead of the door slamming behind me. Things had gone worse than I'd expected. I'd never seen Chris this angry before—at anyone.

I wasn't upset by Chris' rage however, because I blamed myself for his unrealistic and undying faith in Santa. But I share this guilt with…the entire world. Most people in the western hemisphere are a willing part of the Santa scheme, including NORAD (the North American Aerospace Defense Command). About five years before, when our dear friend, Brad Starr, showed Chris NORAD's official Santa Tracker on his computer, it supercharged Chris' faith. Since that time, he had proof beyond merely seeing the red blinking light of an airplane—which he believed to be Rudolf's nose—in the sky each Christmas Eve. Chris had plenty of evidence for his continuing belief in Santa, and I had been a willing co-conspirator.

I left Chris to pout in his room and sat alone in our living room recalling the happy Christmas seasons of my children's early years. They'd enjoyed the many stories I told them about Christmas miracles, such as how St. Nicholas became known as Santa Claus and how he cared individually for all children. My children were confident that Santa personally knew every child in the world and whether his or her actions were good or bad. I happily encouraged their beliefs that every child was important, especially in a world where it might be easy to feel invisible.

When they were younger, my children's faith that

Santa individually knew them was reinforced every year when the special gift they asked for appeared in their stocking or by the tree on Christmas morning. My other kids eventually accepted the truth about Santa without much distress and kindly supported me to keep the magic alive for their brother. I had eagerly maintained the magic of Christmas all those years, never anticipating the future need for hostile combat to end Santa's reign.

"Grinch!" Chris opened his door just to yell at me. His roar jarred me from my nostalgia over Christmases past.

"I'll be up in a minute to talk—everything will be ok, My Buddy." I smiled with the recollection of exactly when Chris got that nickname. It was during Christmas when Chris was just six years old. A year I thought there were too many obstacles for Santa to make it down our chimney.

***

The Christmas of 1984 remains a magical memory for our family—a time when even I believed in Christmas miracles. Although Chris barely spoke any words, I knew he wanted Santa to bring him a doll named "My Buddy," because each time the commercial appeared on TV Chris jumped up and down yelling "My Buddy! My Buddy!" He pointed to a little boy ringing a silver bell while riding on a shiny, candy-apple red bicycle with training wheels. A large doll dressed in a bright red jumpsuit sat balanced between the handlebars with its legs dangling over the front of the bike. The doll looked as charming as his name—My Buddy. Few things made Chris cheerful enough to move at his age, let alone jump up and down. It delighted me to watch him so animated and enthusiastic. I had no choice—when Chris asked Santa to bring him a My Buddy doll for Christmas, of course Santa would!

About two weeks before Christmas I began to panic when I couldn't find the doll at any of the usual toy stores in town. I'd never shopped for a doll made especially for boys before and didn't know how rare they could be. But it didn't take long before I realized I'd need a Christmas miracle to solve my doll dilemma.

Those were the days before online shopping, requiring me to call every drugstore, department store and toy store in town. As my unsuccessful search extended for hours, the geographic search area also extended to neighboring cities. I stopped calling only when I needed to leave for work that evening and resumed my quest as soon as stores opened the next morning.

Finally, I found one toy store two hours away which had one My Buddy doll left in stock—a true Christmas miracle! The store clerk agreed to hold the doll, but only if I promised to arrive before midnight. I explained I had to work until 11:00 pm, but my plea to hold the doll until morning was refused. I desperately called a co-worker who agreed to cover my shift and was pleased to be part of a

Christmas miracle for my son.

As I drove for hours to purchase what was probably the last My Buddy doll in the state, I sang along to the Christmas music on the radio and felt pure happiness, as if I had no problems in my life—another Christmas miracle. The next day, I went to work a tired but peaceful mother, confident all would be merry and bright for my little boy on Christmas morning.

My holiday cheer didn't last long, however. When driving through my neighborhood with Chris in the car a couple of days later, he unexpectedly shouted, "My Buddy!" I looked out the window to see what he pointed at and gasped when I saw a boy riding a red bicycle with training wheels. But there was no doll in sight! Chris grinned as he bounced up and down in his car seat. "My Buddy! My Buddy!"

"Nooooo!" I yelled. "That's a bicycle – not a My Buddy!" But Chris couldn't hear anything I said. The thunder of him kicking his car seat and yelling, "My Buddy!" eclipsed my ability to have any sort of teaching moment.

"Oh, no…Chris! You told Santa you wanted a "My Buddy" *doll* for Christmas – not a bicycle," I tried to control my panic. "You can't change your mind…that's one of Santa's rules! Don't you want a doll?" I begged. My words had no impact. He chanted, "My Buddy!" the rest of the drive home.

When we got into the house, I quickly found a picture of a bicycle in a magazine and showed it to Chris. "My

Buddy!" he yelled again with a broad grin.

I collapsed on the couch and sank into deep despair. With Christmas only a few days away, finding a bicycle— let alone a red bicycle with training wheels, would be impossible. The over-achieving-magic-maker in me had to admit defeat. I thought of my darling six-year-old son, who believed faithfully in Santa, and how hurt he would be on Christmas morning with only a doll beneath the tree. How had I missed the obvious? Chris had never shown any interest in his sister's dolls. The more I thought about it, the more I beat myself up. Why hadn't it occurred to me that Chris would never have asked for a doll for Christmas – even a doll made especially for boys. I needed a serious Christmas miracle this time.

I shared my sad Christmas story with my parents and siblings begging them to keep an eye out for a child's bicycle—in any color. Hours were wasted in a valiant but futile effort to find *any* youth bicycle with training wheels. I even scanned the local newspaper for a used bike before finally relinquishing all hope about three days before Christmas.

I pieced together my broken heart and put on a fake smile as I explained to Chris that Santa's elves might not be able to make a bicycle in time for Christmas, but instead he might get a doll in a red jumpsuit, with a bicycle to come later. Chris seemed unphased and mumbled something I guessed to be about him being on Santa's good list.

Two days before Christmas, my father called me around 8:00 at night. I could barely hear him because of the sounds of people chattering in the background.

"Guess what?" My dad sounded excited.

"What? Where are you?" I was depressed and couldn't muster politeness let alone enough energy to match his enthusiasm.

"Guess!"

"Dad, I'm super tired," I lied. I didn't have enough merry in my Christmas to play any games. "Please, just tell me why you've called."

"You know that miracle you've been hoping for?" he yelled.

I knew exactly what he meant but dared not believe it. "What...a...you mean, you found a child's bike for sale? This close to Christmas?"

"I'm at an auction—a fundraiser for Toastmaster's—and I just outbid everybody on this little bicycle—I think it's the perfect size for Chris. We'll bring it when we come to your house Christmas Eve."

I was stunned. "Oh dad, you're my hero! It's not red, by chance, is it?" I held my breath.

"Bright red bicycle with black training wheels and a silver bell on the handlebar." I sat down on my kitchen floor and cried. Yes! I believed in Christmas miracles.

Waking up before dawn on Christmas morning greeted with the sound of Chris ringing the bell on his new bicycle felt like I was in a Hallmark™ Christmas commercial. I rolled out of bed and pushed open my bedroom door just as Chris rode past me down the hall. He grinned and pointed to his new My Buddy doll sitting between the handlebars. A wave of happiness filled my heart and home that day cementing my belief in Santa's magical influence. That was the day Chris got his nickname and why he'll always be My Buddy.

* * *

Over twenty years had passed since that Christmas of my children's youth, and now it was time to tell Chris the truth about Santa. With two kids in college and large expenses for my other children, money was tight. The responsibilities I carried over the years, together with the cost and exhaustion of the Christmas season dimmed my ability to see any more Christmas miracles. Now, twenty-six year old Chris asking for a frivolous gold Wrestling Belt drained my last ounce of Christmas cheer. I was empty.

Thus began the dark Christmas of 2005—the year I assumed Chris to be old enough to understand the truth. Thus far, my announcement of Santa not being real, only lessened Chris' faith and trust *in me*, not in Santa. I had to finish what I'd started but dreaded any further conversations about Santa. Chris stayed in his room until lunch when I served his favorite turkey sandwich and tried to be cheerful. But he continued to mumble with a defiant scowl each time we made eye contact. He took refuge in his room the rest of the day and sulked through dinner. I began to seriously regret my decision to take on Santa when Chris growled at my offer to sing him a Christmas song and tuck him into bed. He was too heartbroken and angry. When I said, "Goodnight," he glared at me and again mumbled "Santa is weal." With a grunt he rolled over and ignored me in favor of the wall.

The next day brought more of the same battle with Chris giving no indication of softening. My usual loveable teddy bear of a son growled, frowned and stomped away when I tried to soothe his anger or mentioned Christmas. I gave up trying to decipher Chris' grumblings and pretended to ignore him, but occasionally made out words such as "mean, crazy, liar" and "Santa is weal." I needed many gulps of air for courage, but I held the line.

Chris usually forgave quickly, but this anger was a whole new level which I had never seen—not to mention the longest grudge he'd ever held.

The next day we didn't talk about anything Christmas, but his night and dinner prayers turned into a diatribe against me as he pled with God, "Blessma mom…change her heart…tell her Santa is weal." It always surprised me how articulate Chris could be when angry.

Chris flipped from anger to sadness and back again. At bedtime that night when I cautiously asked if I could tuck him in, he merely nodded his agreement—but again he refused a song. I kissed him on the check and whispered to him my promise to keep Santa's spirit alive.

"Santa not dead!" A tear pooled in his eye.

I was battle fatigued. There was no peace on earth or goodwill towards men—or mothers—in our home that Christmas.

When Chris' sister Kathryn called home from college, I hoped things would change.

"Kath! What a relief to talk with someone who is not mad at me!" Chris overheard my excitement and joined me in my room. It made him happy to get calls from his big sisters. He listened intently as I wearily recounted our Santa dispute and miserable beginning of our Christmas. Initially, Kathryn disagreed with my decision, but when I explained his wish for the prohibitively expensive gold belt, her voice softened, and she offered to talk to him.

Confident in Kathryn's ability to get through to Chris and validate my position, I handed Chris the phone. "Your sister wants to talk to you about Santa," I said.

Chris glared at me with an exaggerated frown but as soon as he placed the phone to his ear, he eagerly shared his disgust with me through a jumbled rant of, "Mom is a liar...hates Santa...I'm telling Santa...she'll get lumpa coal...Santa is weal!" And I'm fairly sure I heard a reference to me as "The Grinch."

After Chris ended his complaints, he focused intently. When he began to nod and grin, I had to admit...I was intrigued. His grin seemed to spread through his whole body. He sat up straight and grunted an exuberant, "Uh-huh!"

Chris handed me the phone with a triumphant smile.

"Wow, Kath!" I exclaimed, "You're awesome! What did you say?"

"I told him you were just joking," She chided. "Of course, Santa's real!"

"Ahhhh," I moaned. "I should've known you'd have his back!"

"Mom, you can't take away his happiness at Christmas!" Kathryn scolded. "Remember when I was little and promised you that I would always keep the magic alive for Chris? I haven't forgotten, but I think you have."

Come on Kath, I can't keep this up forever!" I whined.

"Santa's too important to Chris." Her voice softened. "You've gotta give in on this! Chris doesn't have much in his life and you can't take Santa away from him."

"I've always appreciated your love for Chris." I said weakly, but sincerely. I was hopeless and had no fight left in me. "Come home soon and bring us some Christmas cheer," I said dejectedly. I hung up and put my head in my hands. I was surrounded. It was as if I boarded the Polar Express with a one-way ticket to Martyrville.

Chris solemnly nodded his acceptance of my apology and we've never spoken again about whether Santa is real. Luckily—or miraculously—I found a plastic toy Championship Belt for Santa to leave under the tree. It required some modifications to fit Chris, but he didn't seem to care; he was happy just knowing he permanently remained on Santa's good list.

* * *

But Professor Higgins wasn't done helping me to fully understand the true essence of Santa.

Many years later when Chris was thirty-eight, he taught me something unexpected that I wish I'd learned years before—when it could have stopped me from my foolish attempt to take out Santa.

In the Fall of 2016, Chris announced his decision to be Santa Claus for Halloween. I looked at him curiously, as I considered the idea. Throughout my fifty-eight years of Halloweens, I'd never seen anyone in a Santa costume. Chris waited for my expected approval.

"Ummm…I'm not sure you can do that, My Buddy," I said. "I really don't think it would work. People might not be happy."

"You buy Santa suit?" Clearly, Chris and I weren't communicating.

"I'm fairly sure there's an unspoken rule that nobody can dress up as Santa for Halloween. You can't mix holidays." I tried to sound firm, but my protest seemed feeble, even to me.

He insisted, "I am Santa." I changed the subject.

I hoped the impulse had passed, but a few days later he brought the Santa costume up again. Our Santa Battle of 2005 flashed through my mind; I didn't want to open any old wounds. And I always supported his fantasy dreams to become anyone he wished to be on Halloween.

He looked forward to Care-Rite and church Halloween parties and thoughtfully chose his costume every year.

My heart hurt with worry that Chris would not be received well. I didn't want to be a part of anything which could cause Chris to stand out and appear weird or odd—I had spent his entire life focused on avoiding any risk of him being mocked, rejected, or bullied. People might be uncomfortable mixing holiday traditions. Many parents get a little touchy if anyone even hints at exposing the secret alliance protecting the Santa myth.

Over the next few weeks, Chris rejected each of my suggested costuming alternatives. He insisted on dressing as Santa. I considered omitting the wig, beard and glasses for Chris to clearly look like he's only in a partial costume. The predicament presented a tough emotional quandary; I hoped people would notice his Down syndrome features and be tolerant of Chris' desire to impersonate Santa Claus, yet I also worried people would object to a Santa with Down syndrome. But Chris never gave up on his dream.

I bought the suit.

Halloween arrived with a cold, drizzly rain in the morning which matched my mood. I dreaded the parents' anger or shunning of Santa at the church Halloween party that night. I feared teasing from neighborhood trick or treaters even more. After breakfast I invited Chris to go with me to the grocery store. He agreed and surprised me when he came downstairs dressed in his Santa costume.

"We're only getting food at the store, not trick or treating," I said. "Halloween doesn't actually start until tonight when the ghosts and goblins can appear. Let me help you change out of your costume."

Chris shook his head no, patted his big round belly and said, "Ho! Ho! Ho!" He had a twinkle in his eye and the cutest little grin. How could I say no?

"Ok, who cares what time it is, Buddy. It's always Santa time! Let's go." I looked forward to this day being over.

I concealed my embarrassment and ignored the stares as we drove to the store and walked inside. I looked straight ahead and focused on finishing my shopping as quickly as possible.

But Chris had different plans. I heard him shout, "Ho! Ho! Ho!" and looked up to see him waving and strutting as if he were in a parade. Something clicked. I stopped worrying about my embarrassment and focused on enjoying Chris' performance. He was simply charming! Parents pointed him out to their children, "Look, there's someone dressed up as Santa!"

Chris was as natural a Santa as the Jolly Old Elf himself! He patted the children on their heads and mumbled "…good list." He became increasingly animated the longer he performed. Soon he asked me to buy peppermint patties to hand out to kids in the store. I bought several bags! I couldn't wipe the smile off my face as Chris meandered through the aisles stopping to talk to every child we passed. They flocked to him when he handed them candy and their parents seemed delighted by an impromptu Christmas encounter on Halloween.

Yet again, I had underestimated Chris' ability to be the star of the show! He was enrolling everyone, including me, to let Santa join in on the Halloween fun. By the time I checked out with my groceries, my jaw ached from grinning. What a treat to see my son so magnetic around strangers, rather than being invisible. Instead of people averting their eyes away from my son, they treated Chris like a celebrity!

I had never enjoyed Halloween so much and felt overwhelmed with gratitude by the tidal wave of kindness from strangers. Chris was neither an outcast nor odd; he was a cherished part of humanity. It was as if everyone saw the pure goodness in my son's heart, accepted him and were even comfortable letting their kids take candy from him. My time with Santa in the grocery store melted my frozen heart—an early but true Christmas miracle!

While driving home with Santa in the front seat, he gathered more attention. Cars' horns honked and we returned waves from children who eagerly smiled and pointed at Chris through their windows.

My favorite part of our amazing day happened when we stopped at a red light and a teenage boy riding a motorcycle pulled up alongside our car. He looked over at Chris and stared for a moment. Then he lifted his helmet shield and casually said with a serious look, "I want a girlfriend for Christmas." Chris nodded his head, grinned, and gave him up an enthusiastic thumbs up. I smiled broadly and mouthed, "thank you" before driving away.

It must have been the magic in Santa's suit because it cast a similar spell of happiness later at our church Halloween party. All evening Chris enjoyed celebrity status. I giggled when Chris introduced himself as Chris Kringle. I also chuckled when he handed a piece of candy to a young vampire and said, "Be good!"

When we returned home, I recounted the amazing day to my brother, Herb. He loved Halloween but missed that year due to illness. My stories delighted him and soon we were both crying from laughing so hard—but I must admit some of my tears were tears of gratitude for how accepted Chris had been all day. I struggled to find the right words to describe how the caring attention of so many friends and strangers had healed and lifted my heart.

"It was like…It sort of felt like…"

"Like having visions of sugar plums dancing in your head?" Herb said with a slow, wry smile.

"Absolutely!" I replied. We both chuckled.

I laid in bed that night enjoying my memories of the day and recalled Santa Gate of 2005 when I tried to convince my son Santa wasn't real. "Alright!—I was wrong!" I said out loud to nobody listening.

I was warmed by the meaning of the lesson Professor Higgins taught me. Because he mirrored Santa's kindness and caring love for others, he called forth kindness and love from strangers. Thus, he was seen, and he was valued.

Since that day, I have proudly been on Team Santa and will remain so, forever.

LESSON 19
A Shot Of Whisky With A Chaser Of Forgiveness

"**I** drank whiskey," Chris' deep, monotone voice startled me as I stood in my kitchen cutting pie for our guests waiting in the living room. It wasn't only his usually emotionless tone which sounded deeply mournful that shook me, but also…*whiskey? Wait, whaaat?*

I jerked my head around to face him. "What did you say?" His words were unimaginable.

His shoulders were hunched over, and his chin almost touched his chest as he stared at the floor. I reached out and gently raised his chin with my fingers to look directly into his eyes. His obvious sadness immediately broke my heart, but I waited for his reply because I couldn't fathom what I thought I'd just heard.

That moment was the beginning of an extraordinary lesson about how pure love and forgiveness are inextricably entwined.

It was a day or two after Chris' thirty-third birthday.

Explaining how much I loved my son at that point in his life is difficult, other than describing it as perfect, complete and consumed all of me. However, as I stood next to Chris in my kitchen on that warm summer evening in 2011, I felt my love for Chris expand larger than one hundred percent—and learned how my heart's capacity to love had no tangible boundaries.

Our dear friends, Tom and Becky Smith, came over with pie that evening to celebrate Chris' birthday. I left Aubrey and our friends waiting in the living room and had just slipped into the kitchen to dish up some dessert without noticing that Chris had followed me. It was amazing that I didn't drop the pie on the floor when startled by his grave admission.

"Tell me again what you said, My Buddy, I didn't understand." I tried to lift his chin with my fingers to look him in the eyes. Although his words were uncommonly clear, my brain couldn't register them. We were a family that never drank alcohol.

"Idrankwhiskey." This time his woeful voice was just above a whisper. He pulled his head away from my hand, trying to avoid my gaze, but I held his chin firmly and searched his eyes for an explanation. As the shocking confession began to sink in, the scene unfolded in slow motion. I watched tears form in Chris' eyes and saw one large tear begin to trickle down the side of his nose. He wasn't just sad; he was miserable.

Time slowed to a stop as I struggled to accept how his

whiskey-drinking admission could be true. Immediately I felt transported outside of my body, and recall being able to watch the scene from the corner of the room. I could readily see both the shock and confusion on my face as well as Chris' misery on his.

"You drank whisky?" I heard those incredible words tumble out of my mouth.

Chris slowly nodded while maintaining our gaze. He pointed to his single tear. That move usually worked to elicit pity from me, but this time I was too stunned to talk about the tear.

"Are you telling me this because…you're sorry?" I asked delicately, still unable to shake my confusion over what was going on.

Chris closed his eyes and gently nodded.

The adrenalin rush from the reality of what my son was admitting to, whisked me back inside my body. Chris was wretchedly sorrowful about drinking whiskey sometime in his past, and apparently wanted my forgiveness.

I threw my arms around Chris and exclaimed, "You're completely forgiven!" My ardent forgiveness erupted with a jubilant shout—it didn't matter when or why Chris consumed whiskey. What mattered to me was his genuine sorrow for having done so and I wanted only to ease his suffering.

I will never forget the overpowering feeling of love which filled us as we hugged. Jolts of warmth and joy surged through my body. I had never experienced such an explosive expansion of love and joy. There was enough love to fill the entire room and heal both of our hearts at once.

As I stood in the kitchen hugging Chris, my mind quickly shifted to what I had been taught about divine love. I wondered whether God, who loves perfectly and infinitely, might similarly respond when I express genuine remorse for a mistake and desired to change. If God's love could feel anything close to what I felt at that moment, then I knew He shouldn't be feared. Rather, I experienced, firsthand, how His love can lift, heal, and feel wonderful—even joyful. I didn't want the exhilarating feeling to ever leave me. And I wondered where this amazing new depth of love for my son came from.

I lingered with Chris' head on my shoulder and hugged him a little tighter.

A thought hit me—*this must be what it feels like to love in a more Christ-like manner.* I smiled, but then smugly added, *look at me, I am becoming Christ-like.* (Obnoxious, I know.)

Just as quickly as the spirit of sweet forgiveness flooded over me, it immediately drained. My pride had pulled the plug! The warmth and love I had felt vanished, as though an invisible worm hole had opened in my kitchen and pulled all the goodness out.

My jaw tightened with the thought, *who would give whiskey to my sweet, innocent son with Down syndrome?* My heart pounded with rage as names of possible suspects raced through my mind. The fact that Chris was legally old enough to be served alcoholic drinks didn't matter a whit to me because I made the decision to raise my kids in an alcohol free lifestyle. And Chris never showed any interest in trying alcohol. Someone had to have pranked my son! There could be no other explanation. And I absolutely planned to hold that someone accountable—he or she would suffer my wrath to ensure it never happened again!

Who was the reckless punk that gave whiskey to my son? I screamed inside my head: *I'm going to kill 'em!* The pool of suspects was narrow. Since Chris didn't spend time with many young adults outside of his work program, I knew the perpetrator had to be one of his siblings or one of their friends. Adrenalin stoked my rage with each potential suspect I considered.

I pulled back from our embrace to look Chris directly in his eyes. I mustered as much self-control as possible to smile and feign a kind voice. "Buddy, when did you drink whiskey? Who was with you?"

"At Dad's wedding."

MY EX-HUSBAND! He gave my innocent son whiskey! Chris didn't say exactly *who* handed him the drink(s), *but of course, my Ex had to be the culprit!* I slowly and loudly breathed in the thought, welcoming oxygen to stoke the flames of anger surging through my body—even my toes were incensed.

What a low life! Even if Chris accidentally drank from

glasses set out for the wedding toast, did my Ex not have enough class to serve champagne like everyone else? What was the theme of the wedding—a wild west saloon? How tacky! I could feel the heat in my face from the flames of fury blazing inside me. Since the wedding happened several weeks prior, I wondered whether Chris had been in misery all that time while waiting to tell me of his indiscretion.

My outrage abruptly ended, however, when Chris added, "Aubrey drank whiskey too!" With those words, the emotional roller coaster I was riding careened off the tracks. Aubrey was the only family member whom I hadn't considered to be involved in Chris' confessed drunken incident. I completely trusted my twenty-one year-old daughter and was confident she would not drink whiskey, even if served at their father's wedding. She most certainly would've never allowed Chris to even taste it without calling me first. I gasped for air and sighed loudly with relief as I slumped into a kitchen chair. I was exhausted from the emotional roller coaster ride.

"Aubrey," I called out to her in the living room, "can you come in here for a moment to help me?" After she stepped into the room, I smiled at her with raised eyebrows. "Chris just told me he drank whiskey with you at your father's wedding."

"Of course not!" Aubrey blurted out even before I finished the sentence. She shot Chris a furious glance. We both knew Chris had a propensity to throw her under the bus when he was worried about getting in trouble. After all, she was always the little sister in his eyes. Chris looked at her nervously and shrugged his shoulders as if to say, "Sorry, but we're in this together."

Feeling sorry for Aubrey as I saw the color drain from her face, I quickly added, "I know you wouldn't drink whiskey with Chris. But why would he say it happened?"

"We toasted my Dad's marriage with non-alcoholic champaign that he had especially for us!" Aubrey shot another angry look at Chris before explaining, "I remember thinking at the time how weird it was that he was drinking out of the bottle! I had an odd feeling when I saw him carrying the bottle around the dance floor and acting silly, but I figured he was just playing around. Now I get it. He must've thought he was drunk." Aubrey and I looked at each other with a knowing smile and she relaxed.

"Buddy, your sister is right. You didn't drink whiskey at your dad's wedding. Your dad made sure there was special juice just for his kids. You're fine." I said quietly, being completely drained from the emotional whiplash I had just experienced.

"Hmh." Chris seemed both surprised and relieved by my assurance he had nothing to be forgiven for. However, there is a fair possibility he still believes his bottle contained whiskey and he got away with his—first and only—drunken escapade. Either way, our extended family survived Chris' confession, and we've grown closer as we laugh about this memory.

We rejoined our guests in the living room and apologized for the length of time we took to serve dessert. I'm sure I looked exhausted after my journey through so many emotions in such a brief period of time.

Later that night I sat in my family room, alone and reviewed the evening. I was relieved that there had never been a whiskey issue but felt as if I had survived a near death by drowning in a sea of confusing emotions. I felt guilty for my judgments and anger, gratitude for my awesome daughter to have taken such diligent care of Chris, and even admiration for my ex-husband and his new wife for making sure there were non-alcoholic drinks for my children to join in their toast.

No lectures about forgiveness could've been more transformational than the lessons Professor Higgins taught me that evening. Because I felt it. I know that forgiveness is based on pure love, not on self-righteousness and making others wrong.

I saw how Chris' vulnerability and humility to admit mistakes made him more loveable, not less. His remorse triggered my sincere desire to help heal his wounded heart, not to hurt him further.

I contemplated my contradictory reactions and found it interesting that I willingly forgave Chris but refused forgiveness to anyone I thought had taken advantage of him, including my other children. What a paradox! I genuinely loved them too! Was it because of Chris' innate innocence that I hadn't harshly judged his whiskey drinking? Did I consider him to be pure of heart and incapable of intentionally making a wrong decision? Why didn't I view my other children or their friends in the same light? I realized it was *my judgments* about the capabilities and motives of the imagined perpetrators which determined my reactions. And I had misjudged them all.

I was embarrassed by my harsh judgments. Shame usually feels so horrible that I bury it, but this time it prompted me to seek forgiveness because I knew how wonderful and loving forgiveness can be.

The way Professor Higgins taught me about how love and forgiveness are entwined was transformative in my life. I wanted to experience more of those light, warm, blissful feelings of acceptance and inner healing. I was clear that pride and judgment created anger and contempt which felt dark, heavy and exhausting.

I learned that forgiveness stems from pure love and is judgment free. When suspending my judgment, I can be more concerned about others than myself and forgiveness comes naturally.

Additionally, I discovered how pride blocks divine love. When my focus shifted from caring about Chris to complimenting myself about my supposed charitable reaction, my pride turned into a vacuum which sucked all the love from my heart…and the entire room. Anger and hate immediately and effortlessly filled the emptied space.

Since that whiskey confession by Professor Higgins in my kitchen so many years ago, I've changed. After feeling the extreme power of love—without pride or judgment— which produced forgiveness, I have been propelled to forgive freely and to seek forgiveness quickly.

(Of course, I don't mean to understate the need for boundaries to be set in place in cases of genuine circumstances of harm when forgiving others. That subject was merely not part of these lessons.)

I've learned how forgiveness can transform the giver even more than the receiver because it opened space in my life for more love and happiness. I now appreciate why those who understand pure love earnestly seek opportunities to forgive.

The Humanity Quotient: Another Way To Measure Intelligence

At the beginning of each school year, I attended planning meetings to set Chris' educational goals and was given copies of medical and educational reports written by experts who referred to Chris' low Intelligence Quotient (IQ) scores. The teachers and experts routinely relied on the IQ score to evidence my son's low cognitive abilities when establishing goals and expectations for the upcoming year.

But the number wasn't meaningful to me. I instinctively knew not to give a lot of credit to a numerical measurement of my son's capabilities. I disagreed with the use of psychometrics and the application of statistical methods as a comprehensive way to evaluate my son. I never believed that IQ tests could fairly calculate human diversity. Chris didn't have the strong verbal skills which IQ tests required for relaying abilities to solve problems. And how can intelligence be accurately predicted at the early age of five or seven—when he was initially evaluated? I stopped caring about Chris' IQ scores early in his school years.

I also intuitively understood that Chris' cognitive functioning may not be as valuable to society as his other strengths, such as his love, empathy and ability to make people happy. Chris has a way of making people feel seen, loved and important with few to no words and sometimes with only a wink, a smile or a thumbs up.

These innate abilities shined brilliantly during a family trip to celebrate Chris' fortieth birthday in New York City. It had been one of Chris' biggest dreams for a long time to visit Brooklyn where the story took place in his beloved Disney movie, *The Newsies*. He had watched the movie over and over and blasted the soundtrack during family road trips for years.

During our taxi ride from JFK Airport to our hotel in midtown Manhattan I was charmed by Chris's excitement as he looked down every street. I was sure he was hoping to see a newspaper boy peddling papers or carrying a picketing banner.

Our driver's heavy accent piqued my curiosity, so I introduced ourselves and asked him where he was from and how long he had lived in New York. He introduced himself as John and explained that he had moved from Hong Kong about ten years earlier, when he was about forty years old.

I shared that we were in town to celebrate my son's

birthday. He looked at Chris and mirrored his contagious smile as he asked what we planned to do while in town. Chris continued to look out the window and I explained Chris' wish to be the king of New York. John kindly became our tour guide and shared interesting facts about each part of the city we passed through, but his accent was so heavy that I continuously struggled to understand him. I needed to watch his mouth in the rear view mirror to decipher most of his words. He drove through the Queens-Midtown Tunnel and told us about the tubes under the East River. He pointed out the United Nations complex and Grand Central Terminal, which he described as the largest train station in the world.

As we drove, I asked John many questions about his experiences living in two mega cities and found his stories fascinating. I kept looking at Chris to see if he understood any of John's stories, but Chris appeared blissfully immersed in the sights from his window and the diverse sounds of the city. He didn't utter one word the entire drive, but never stopped grinning. I assumed Chris couldn't understand anything John was saying, so I just let him be.

During our forty-five minute drive, I was impressed by John's courage and resilience, and expressed my sincere admiration for his ability to successfully create a new life in such a complicated, expensive city. John nodded and smiled.

After arriving at our hotel, Chris and I stood at the

curb while John retrieved our luggage from the trunk. When John was done, Chris stepped over to face him, straightened his back, placed his palms together in front of his heart and slowly bowed.

"Shay Shay," Chris said.

I looked quizzically at Chris and then back at John who grinned broadly as he excitedly replied to Chris in a foreign language which neither Chris nor I understood. But Chris didn't miss a beat and bowed lowly a second time.

John's face beamed. I saw his eyes light up as he stood a little taller. He returned a bow to Chris and continued speaking in the same language. I didn't know what either of them said or what language they spoke, but I felt something peaceful bridge the space between them. I also felt awkward, a little like an outsider who had not been invited to the party.

"Um…what did…a…you just say…um…to my son?" I asked.

"He said, 'thank you' and I said, you're welcome!" John explained. Still grinning, he looked back at Chris and held his gaze.

"Were you both speaking in Chinese?" I asked. Chris talking in a foreign language was incomprehensible and stupefied me. I looked back and forth at them and studied their faces. All I could do was pause and breath the moment in. I felt uplifted by the tangible bond of kindness and mutual respect shared between them.

After John and I exchanged good-byes—in English—I patted Chris on the back with pride. As soon as John drove away, I turned to my son and questioned with astonishment, "How do you know how to say thank you in Chinese?"

Chris blinked at me in silence for a moment and then casually said, "Jackie Chan."

I threw my hand up in disbelief at the simplicity of his answer. I thought he probably wanted to add, *"Who doesn't know* how to say thank-you in Chinese? Jackie Chan taught it to the entire world in his *Rush Hour* movies."

I was awestruck by my son who rarely speaks—and when he does talk, he uses only a limited vocabulary. He not only knew people from Hong Kong speak Chinese, but also how to show respect for John by thanking him in his own language. Wow! I was humbled by my own inadequacy. I had seen all the same Jackie Chan movies Chris had—although not as many times—but regrettably I had apparently not cared enough to memorize how to say thank you in Chinese.

When we got to our room, I sat and considered the amazing encounter my bilingual Buddy and I had with John. I mistakenly thought Chris had not been paying attention to our driver as he sat in silence. I had assumed he was wrapped up in the stimulation of New York City and had completely missed his excitement about meeting someone from Hong Kong.

The way I tried to show my respect for John was by caring enough to ask questions about his life and relocation to America. He was friendly and seemed receptive to my questions because he shared many personal stories. But with one gesture and two words, my son made a much more positive impact on our new friend. Chris showed sincere respect and love by speaking John's language.

In that moment I finally understood the significance of the advice my mom had given me many times, "It's not what you say, but how you say it and how you treat people which makes all the difference." Chris made a difference in the world that day; he not only lifted John's mood, but also inspired me to be better.

Throughout our trip (and many times afterwards), I reminisced about the valuable insight I gleaned from my experience with Chris and John. Unexpectedly, memories flashed through my mind of Chis as a baby when I worried whether he would be capable enough to make a difference in the world. I was awfully naive back then. I wished I could go back in time and brag about Chris' accomplishments that day to prior school professionals who marginalized Chris' capabilities and brain power based on an IQ score. I would tell them there were many more important skills than solving random logic problems on some narrowly drawn, standardized test. Chris has shown me that his intelligence is far too complex to be precisely measured by tests.

I smiled thinking about the juxtaposition of our educa-tion—me, with a doctorate degree and various titles and awards, compared to Chris with his Special Education certificate (not even a high school diploma). But standing on a curb in New York City that summer day, it was Chris who outperformed me in communicating our respect to John.

Chris was born to teach. He is a living demonstration of why an IQ score may not be a wholly accurate way of measuring intellect. Chris understands happiness. And he has the wisdom of sensing what would make individual people happy, even though it varies between different people—like saying "you're cool" to a gang member in Walmart, or "Xie Xie" to John. Chris also has the intuition to know what would make large groups of people happy—like acting as the star of the show—no matter how small the role—or handing out peppermint patties while dressed as Santa for Halloween. And much of his instinct likely aligns with what makes Chris happy—being seen and understood, being treated like he's special (but not "special"), being valued for wanting to take care of those he loves, and when people enjoy his pranks or give him direct and genuine attention for his acting, singing, etc. Chris is masterful at giving to others what makes him feel loved. I call that a type of profound emotional intelligence that even so-called "geniuses" identified by IQ tests, somehow fail to achieve.

A better way to assess the type of intelligence Chris

demonstrates—the loving care and dignified treatment of others—would be a Humanity Quotient (HQ), which is most important and needful in our world today. With a natural understanding of unconditional love and a high capacity for empathy, social understanding, and the ability to lift others, Chris' HQ score is remarkably high.

I welcomed this lesson into my life. Since that day in New York City, I have been motivated to show my respect to my fellow travelers on this shared planet by learning to say at least a few essential phrases in their native language, such as "Hello," "thank you," and "pardon me." My pronunciation may not be perfect, but if Chris can try, so can I.

Xie Xie Ni for this fine lesson, Professor Higgins.

LESSON 21
Love Is The Ultimate Superpower

The extra chromosome Chris rocks might just be a concentrated shot of unconditional love gifted to him from the Universe. This character trait is often mentioned when describing many people with Trisomy 21. I have heard numerous lucky family members consistently describe their relative with Down syndrome to be "extraordinarily loving."

I've never held myself out to be an expert on love, and humbly admit there is much for me to learn from Chris about this virtue. Love is Chris' superpower. He and those like him are essential because love for each other is what protects humanity from hopelessness.

I struggle to find suitable words to describe the way Chris offers love to others. Although my words don't do justice to the power of his unadulterated love, I venture forward because this book would be defectively incomplete without addressing Chris' greatest strength. It would be unfair not only to him but also to the human family to omit his teachings about love.

On countless occasions I've seen Chris' love touching those around him. I know some attributes of his love superpower; it is simple, pure, and unconditional. It is the quintessence of feeling accepted and of being held in a state of grace. It raises spirits, softens hearts and heals emotional wounds. Indeed, it has the power to change the lives of those who choose to receive it.

His siblings describe him as having a calming presence. I've seen how he lifts his siblings and their spouses as they work through frustrations in raising their children. If he thinks they're upset, he gently touches their shoulder, tries to make them smile or supports them with a tender, "You're agoodmom," or "You're astar." Because of Chris' authenticity they know his compliments are based in truth.

There were many times tensions were high in our home while his siblings were young. Chris often approached anyone yelling with a gentle rebuke of "be nice to ma mom," or "be nice to ma sista." (He's chastised me many times in this way.) His example of standing up for others in a loving way softened our hearts. And his ability to live in the reality of each moment helped everyone to feel seen and valued. We knew that he cared about each one of us, so when he stood up for another family member by asking us to be kinder, we knew it was the right thing to do.

When she described Chris' tender heart and its influence on her, his sister Aubrey said, "I know Chris is extremely sensitive to contention—I've seen how the slightest raise in my voice can hurt his heart, requiring me to change the way I speak to him. His constant reminder to be gentle and lead with kindness has helped me heal. As I've changed my perspective to see the good in others, it is easier to give them the benefit of the doubt that they're doing their best at the moment. I've become kinder and gentler with myself as well."

An old, sage saying which reminds me of Chris teaches that "you cannot pour from an empty cup." In Chris' case, his cup is continuously overflowing. And with a "pay it forward" mindset we all have received enough love to freely share.

With Chris' powerful lessons on love constantly around me, I wonder why this lesson has been so difficult for me to explain. Perhaps I haven't learned enough about unconditional love. Is it *my* issue? If so, what is the issue? My eyes involuntarily roll towards the ceiling and I both laugh and grimace recalling the many times Chris asked God in our family prayers to change my heart. And to drive home his point, whenever singing one of his favorite Disney tunes, he routinely pointed to me when the song mentioned having a frozen heart. I gnashed my teeth and pretended to ignore him. But perhaps in this regard I stand with many members of the human family who expect love to fit our expectations and designs, instead of being unconditional about the diverse types of love offered to us. In other words, I've needed to learn a lot.

Truth is, through most of his life, Chris has known me as a self-reliant, single parent who focused on results more than relationships. I was so busy providing life's necessities for my family I didn't have time to indulge all my feelings. I put off dating to raise six strong-willed, independent and highly "individual" children (including Chris). Essentially, Chris' prayers were fitting. I had built walls around my heart and felt safe in my world of invulnerability.

One evening as I sat in front of my computer typing the tenth re-write of this chapter, I was deep in thought about why I was experiencing such a profound writer's block about this lesson. By this time, I was sure my inability to describe Chris' loving influence had to be my issue, because clearly it wasn't his. My efforts to share what I've learned from Professor Higgins about love is like the Titanic's Captain lecturing on understanding icebergs.

Suddenly, a soft touch on my shoulder jostled me back to reality. My forty-four-year-old teddy bear of a son interrupted yet another session of self-deprecation as he leaned in for a hug. He placed one arm on my back, reached around the front of me with his other arm and gave me a long, gentle, bear hug. He nestled his head between my neck and shoulder for an extra moment and mumbled, "I luff ya Mama. Yor a goodmom."

"Ahhh," I sighed and drew in a deep breath. Love poured into my heart, with the overflow trickling as tears down my cheeks. Did he know? How could he possibly know I was writing about love—my most difficult of life lessons? But he did know.

"Thank you, My Buddy. You're my hero."

Chris smiled, said nothing else and went back to his room to watch *The Newsies* for the seven thousandth time.

I recognized that same peaceful but powerful feeling from other precious moments with Chris. It's the same feeling I have every time he randomly calls me on the phone and serenades me with, *"You Are So Beautiful to Me,"* or *"What a Wonderful World"*—he even calls from another room when we are both in the house. My heart melts in his sunshine.

Immediately I focused inward to capture what I was feeling. My heart was flying freely above the world in a universe beyond earthly cares. I realized again, what I've learned and relearned, thanks to Chris—nothing else matters, compared to love.

And that's where true change begins. With a freshly thawed heart, I started over on writing this lesson. Appropriately, Chris' pure love facilitates do-overs. It allows space for beginnings and inspires an open heart. Professor Higgins has repeatedly taught me that when I am vulnerable enough to receive love, I become invested with a desire to start over—to shift my thoughts and perspective to do better, to improve how I see others and to be gentler with myself.

Part of this lesson involves reciprocity. Chris perpetually gives and receives love. I consider myself one of the luckiest mothers in the world to have Chris in my family and I know his siblings all feel the same. There were many occasions while raising my family when I tried to hide my feelings of sadness, discouragement or loneliness. Chris would sense my feelings and show up near me. He'd sit down nearby and simply look at me. He often hugged me spontaneously, but sometimes he waited for me to reach over and stroke his hair or scratch his back. If I took too long to respond to his presence, he scooted closer and sort of nuzzled in until I could no longer ignore him. Inevitably, when I put my arm around him or stroked his arm, *I felt better.* On those occasions, he rarely said anything—his loving presence was enough to heal me.

Simple, pure love has the power to create miracles. For instance, when I am too sick to get out of bed Chris sits nearby holding my hand and with an occasional kiss, whispers, "Don't die." The healing power of his love is palpable, prompting my promise to quickly recover.

Just because my family has been given this gift of an open portal to constant love doesn't mean we haven't experienced sadness or tough times. Even with Chris' loving influence, our family life wasn't always rainbows and butterflies. We had our normal share of discord, especially when his siblings were teenagers. Although we were free to disagree with each other and sometimes argue, nobody in the family ever said a harsh word to

Chris. *Except for one time* when Chris was about twenty-seven years old. And no one in the family has ever forgotten that dreary day.

The infamous incident happened on a sweltering summer evening when Tara was 40 weeks pregnant. As explained earlier, both Tara and Kathryn have been marvelous sisters to Chris. They're only one and two years younger, but he looked to them as big sisters and caregivers. They didn't just mother him, they went out of their way to include and entertain him. They were vigilant at school and around friends to ensure nobody every spoke a harsh word to him or teased him.

After dinner that day, everyone but Chris and I were gathered in the family room. Although I didn't witness the scene, I overheard the worst of it. Tara saw Chris sneak into the kitchen through another room for a third plate of pizza. (Chris had fine-tuned the art of covert pizza-nabbing.)

"Chris, you've had enough. No more!" she commanded. (She worried about his insatiable appetite for pizza and his weight.) Chris pretended not to hear—his customary response to any orders which pertained to food—and piled more pizza on his plate.

"Mom!" I heard Tara yell, "Chris is getting his sixth piece of pizza. You need to say something!"

"My Buddy, that's enough pizza," I yelled from my desk. "Are you *really* still hungry?"

"Uh huh," Chris grunted.

"OK, but only one more piece," I said as I walked into the family room just in time to see Chris look at Tara with a champion's glare and heard him sing tautingly, "Hee Hee Hee Hee." I froze in shock—and fear—upon seeing Tara's face turn bright red and her eyes flash with anger. She spit out sounds and tried to bite back words at the same time, with her fury finally erupting with a shouted insult, "CHUBBY!"

Chris froze. We all froze with raised brows and our eyes fixed on Tara. Chris might not have known what the word meant, but he could tell by Tara's explosion that it had to be bad. Nobody moved or spoke for a long moment as we wondered what to say. Not one of us had ever heard anyone call Chris a hurtful name. But nobody dared to poke the beast.

Tara's hand shot up and covered her mouth as she gasped in horror over the insult. Her eyes bulged with shocked guilt. Chris' jaw dropped and his eyes opened wide, fixed on Tara. Jared and Kathryn remained frozen, staring at Tara. Aubrey sank back into her seat to hide from any other verbal attacks. I was embarrassed—sure I had caused the contention by indulging Chris, and feared saying anything would inflame the situation.

It was our dragon slayer, Jason, who saved the day. "Wow, Tara! You really need to get that baby out!"

Tara's face contorted. "I'm so sorry! I can't believe I said that!" Her agony shifted our shock into nervous laughter. Chris gave Tara a forgiving wink and darted out of the kitchen to his bedroom with his cache of pizza.

Chris doesn't hold grudges (except for a *long* few days during Santa Gate). It's simply not part of his nature. He is always quick to forgive and move forward in happiness and peace. And this, I've learned, is the nature of real love.

Since true love allows for do-overs, its magic turned this dreadful situation into extra love and happiness in our home. After Tara apologized to everyone, we laughed with empathy for her pregnancy misery. There was no retaliation or desire for punishment. Chris' influence has inspired everyone in the family to try again to keep claiming our best selves.

Almost twenty years have passed since that day, but the story has become even more entertaining whenever her siblings tease Tara to "Be nice. Don't be mean... remember that time you called Chris 'chubby?'" Instead of escalating, the caution always invokes laughter.

Most people with Down syndrome as well as their family members report an elevated level of happiness in their lives. Chris is clearly one of those stats. It might be easy to simply assume Chris' happiness arises out of a lack of emotional depth or from an inability to feel rejected, abused or depressed. Not so.

Rather, Professor Higgins has taught me how happiness emerges from love when seeing the good in others, when forgiving amid hurt and moving forward with starting over. (If applicable, to starting over with boundaries or new expectations in place.)

I am happy to report that Chris no longer claims I have a frozen heart, and his current prayers include his thanks for my "changed heart." Therefore, I must be a successful graduate from this course on love. Although I still consider myself a work in progress.

Either way, it has been a great privilege to have received such an enlightening education about pure, unconditional love from our pizza-nabbing Professor Higgins.

WORK/LIFE EXPERIENCE

LESSON 22

Creating A Win/Win Is A Work Of Heart

"**B**less ma mom—be good warrior." Chris prayed. His words startled me.

A warrior? I'd heard him pray to bless me in my work many times, but apparently, I'd never listened closely enough to notice his mispronunciation of the word "lawyer." I joked to myself, *Huh, maybe that's why it seems I'm always fighting for everything—perhaps his prayers are why I'm not much of a peacemaker. Chris has been praying for me to be a good warrior for as long as I've been an attorney.*

We were all gathered in my master bedroom on that beautiful California spring evening when Chris was about thirty-two years old. Chris often volunteered to offer our family prayers. Since our prayers are unscripted, he enjoyed the "open mic" opportunity and regularly included requests to bless each of us in personal and thoughtful ways. Sometimes he simply wanted to express his opinions without interruption.

After the prayer I gave him a hug. "Buddy, your mom is a *lawyer*, not a warrior." I slowly repeated, "la-la-lawyer."

Chris studied my face and repeated, "wa-wa-warrior," with a confident nod of his head as if to say, "I got it."

I held out little hope my correction would be effective because Chris' enlarged tongue made it difficult for him to enunciate the letter 'L.' I chuckled again, wondering if there was merit to my initial theory that the zealous way I acted had something to do with his many prayers.

In truth, I *was* a warrior. I saw my role as a litigator to be like a crusader preparing for mental combat. Although I simply thought of myself as a professional advocate for my client's interests, I had to admit I could also be a fierce combatant when necessary. I not only loved winning, but also enjoyed the art of battle itself and dedicated myself to do whatever work was necessary to prevail. I took pride in the reputation I had gained in my office by tackling hopeless causes, employing novel strategies and obtaining victories in court.

Later that evening, as I tucked Chris into bed, I paused for a moment and reflected on his perspective of my job in comparison to the loving way he interacts with the world around him. I worked in an environment demanding an analytical, logical, unemotional, right/wrong, winner take-all mentality which doesn't generally prioritize caring about people and especially not their feelings. I wondered how my career could be impacted if I applied the lessons Professor Higgins taught me about empathy, listening, accepting, seeing the good in others and leading with my heart. Lawyering in Chris mode was a foreign concept to me. And his tendency to live in the present afforded the luxury of authentic spontaneity which would not fit well in a legal workplace. To be as polished as possible, most of my work was thoroughly contemplated and scripted.

And, as a female, I was keenly aware of how the legal profession originated as a man's world and how diligently my female colleagues and I worked to break through the glass ceiling. I had spent over twenty years—my entire career—avoiding appearing emotional or too sensitive. In the business and legal world, expressing feelings is usually taboo and gentleness is often misinterpreted as weakness. Leading with my heart would be foreign territory indeed.

I dismissed the possibility of living the way Chris does as being unrealistic—he didn't live in my world where we all need to fight to succeed. I ended my ponderings with a good laugh at the silly notion that Chris' word play had any influence on the way I navigated my career.

But after years of tutelage from my Professor Higgins, I *had* changed. A few days later, I was surprised by the unexpected lesson which surfaced. At the time, I was involved in a high-stakes real estate litigation regarding the development of a large industrial park. Several prestigious law firms were involved in the matter, some represented prominent environmental groups (those protecting endangered species), others represented concerned citizens (objectors), as well as attorneys for the landowners and the developer. I was the sole attorney representing the County government in enforcing its land use regulations at the heart of the case.

After months of negotiations and legal discovery, there appeared to be no hope for a mutual resolution of the lawsuit. Thus, the court set a deadline for all attorneys to "meet and confer" and submit briefs outlining which issues, if any, could be resolved prior to trial. As I worked late into the night reviewing the issues in preparation for the settlement conference, I realized little had been resolved despite the plethora of legal eagles and the many hours billed on the case.

My client, the County, was right in the middle of a fierce dispute between the citizen environmental groups who alleged the county's regulations were too lenient to protect the endangered kangaroo rat in the area and the developers and landowners who argued that the County's regulations were unreasonable, overly burdensome and too expensive. They argued that the development would bring productivity and many jobs to the region. Because of the diverse and polarized desires of the parties and minimal progress in the case, the judge encouraged all parties to compromise on as many minor issues as possible.

Like the other attorneys, I tried to appear in settlement conferences prepared to out-strut the other legal peacocks in the room. To appear as a polished professional, I prepared a script with powerful, precise words which would best support my arguments and theories. All my ducks would be in a row to avoid any surprises which could throw me off my game.

The morning of the settlement conference in this case, I sat quietly in the conference room waiting for all counsel to be seated at the table. Instead of my usual strong, energetic self, I was fatigued. In addition to early morning mother duties, I had just been assigned another huge case with imminent deadlines. I don't know what came over me—but something in me shifted. I started the meeting and surprised everyone, including myself, with my opening comments:

"Gentlemen,"—I was the only woman in the room— "before we begin, may I take a minute to share a personal thought?" Heads turned and everyone stared at me in silence. I had never shared a personal story with this group of colleagues; our cordial interactions had been strictly professional. Those who were standing moved to take a seat at the long conference table.

"You may find what I'm about to say to be unusual, but I feel compelled to share an experience I had with one of my children the other night. I have the privilege of being the mother of a thirty-five-year-old son who is diagnosed with Down syndrome, a condition which affects his ability to speak clearly."

Silence continued to fill the room, but now it was more palpable. Nobody moved, and I didn't pause to interpret their blank stares. My mouth was being led by my heart and my brain was merely watching the show.

"In our family prayers the other night my son asked God to bless his mother to be a good *warrior*. He has difficulty articulating the sound of the letter 'L,' but his words caught my attention and I laughed, realizing how zealously I tend to fight when representing my clients' interests. After his prayer, I corrected him explaining, I am a la-lawyer, not a wa-warrior."

I looked around the room and noticed everyone staring either at me or down at their papers on the table. The silence grew awkward, and I wanted to bolt from the room. But I dared not show my nervousness and knew the only way out of this uncomfortable situation was to power through it. So, I continued.

"I hold each of you in high esteem. Everyone at this table has been a keen advocate in fighting for your client's best interests. But gentlemen, today I propose we lean away from being warriors. Cumulatively, we cost thousands of dollars per hour, and we've spent far too much of our clients' money over the past several months to show such little progress towards a resolution. We've seen what great warriors can do. I propose we be great *lawyers* today and resolve this case. Let's figure out ways to compromise and settle this in the best interests of everyone."

We sat in pin-drop silence for what seemed too long. I assumed the other attorneys had to be stunned by this drastic deviation from my usual demeanor. I was way off script and immediately became concerned I could have offended some by mentioning God. I worried I could have tanked my reputation.

However, the others couldn't have been more dismayed by my words than I was! As the moments stretched on, I began to seriously second guess myself. I drew in a deep breath as quietly as possible and shuffled through my files on the table to hide any doubt in my eyes. I could feel a moan of agony rising inside me which I forced back down with a hard swallow.

I had never shared anything this personal with opposing counsel before. I was immediately embarrassed to have been so vulnerable. In one fell swoop I mentioned being a mother, shared my son's medical diagnosis and challenges, and mentioned God and prayers. Religion was almost a forbidden subject for me to bring up because I represented the government and had a constitutional duty to support the separation of church from state, so I always steered clear of any reference to God. I felt my shoulders droop under the weight of the heavy silence in the room. Finally, it was interrupted by an attorney sitting directly across from me.

"Wow! Ms. Smith, those words packed a powerful punch!" I quickly looked up and hoped I hid my relief to see him smile. "I'm sorry to hear about your son's condition." He turned to the lawyer sitting next to him and said, "Wasn't that exceptional insight?"

The other attorney slowly nodded while in deep

thought. I thought I saw a glimmer of respect in his eyes. The attorney to my left said, "Why not?"

Someone else voiced, "Let's do this!"

Lawyers turned to each other and simultaneously engaged in multiple conversations. I remained in silence, and as I made eye contact with others around the room, I welcomed more nods. After an hour or so of rehashing issues and making phone calls to key clients, we were proud to note considerable progress and concluded the meeting with a mutual resolve to draft a compromise and enroll our respective clients to support it.

At the end of our meeting, I silently breathed in the scent of mutual respect mixed with camaraderie and brilliance. What had I done? This was a new moment for me—bringing in wisdom to my work which I'd gained from my son. I wish I could have started my legal career more akin to this manner.

Seven months of unproductive negotiations ended two weeks later when a Settlement Agreement was signed by all parties and submitted to the court.

The tutoring I received from Professor Higgins inspired a meaningful change in my work on this case. Although delivered in an unusual manner, the common denominator of everything he has taught me has been to remember to open my heart and see new possibilities. This time it was to learn the importance of being more of a lawyer than a warrior.

Not only did the attorneys work respectfully and professionally in resolving this case, but afterwards I also noticed a change in the way many of the citizens interacted with the property owners and developers. During future public hearings there was notably less hostility and increased respect for each other.

This case turned out uniquely different. By listening with empathy to the desires of all parties in the action—to not only see others' perspectives, but also to understand and respect their philosophies and values, the focus shifted from legal battle strategies to problem solving with a win/win attitude.

It was as if humanity had been the real winner in the case.

Who Gets A Ventilator?
The Case For Professor Higgins

Some people crochet for fun, some paint, others play pickleball. I watch the news. Good or bad, I want to know what's going on around me and throughout the world. My kids might call that being an obsessive know-it-all, but I consider it being well-informed. We all cope with this complicated, challenging world in our own way.

In late 2019 and early 2020, my part-time hobby escalated into a full-blown obsession as I closely followed world news about the Coronavirus (CoVid) pandemic surging through Europe and eastern countries. Pleas for medical supplies, specifically protective gear and medical grade ventilators initially, poured out from overwhelmed and under-resourced hospitals in China, Russia and Italy. News of this fast spreading virus causing severe lung damage was dreadful. Even worse were the resulting masses of gravely ill patients with high percentages of deaths. Global faith in the medical community was rocked to its core. And the lack of medical equipment (specifically ventilators) in hospitals shocked everyone.

I read daily press updates and watched the news from multiple sources—as much as four heart-sickening hours a day—about overburdened doctors, the misery of nurses and support staff struggling to compensate for inadequate medical supplies and overcrowded emergency rooms. Boiling deep underneath my concern for the world's suffering, however, was my personal terror about whether this plague might come to America and pose a risk to my family members' lives (and particularly my son's).

The news about the symptoms, how easily it spread, and the high mortality rates triggered my worst fears that my forty-two-year-old son could catch pneumonia from this virus. Some thought I was overreacting, but abnormalities of the immune system associated with Down syndrome can sometimes cause an increased susceptibility to respiratory illnesses. And Chris had been prone to catching pneumonia from simple cold/flu viruses. I didn't know how CoVid would affect him.

Could this medical nightmare happen to us? I had never imagined living in a world where my son couldn't get adequate medical care, when needed. And several countries were announcing that very scenario—the lack of supplies to help their virus-infected patients to breathe.

Medical experts on the pandemic's front lines spoke cryptically as governments failed to provide enough needed supplies, but some bravely publicized their hellish dilemma: being forced to select which patient would get a respirator while another would not. Many patients died in emergency rooms while waiting for a ventilator or even before receiving a hospital bed.

Late one night I was in my room watching a chilling BBC interview with a doctor in Russia struggling to explain his colleague's death from falling out of a fifth story window in a veteran's hospital. His beleaguered expression, gaunt cheeks and the dark moons under his eyes reflected the fatigue and agony in his voice. His eyes skittered around the room as he hesitantly answered the reporter's questions pointed at the suspicious nature of the doctor's death. He explained that the deceased doctor had been outspoken against the Russian government for failing to provide adequate medical supplies and personnel for proper treatment, resulting in significant numbers of patient deaths.

I jumped out of bed, stood close to the TV carefully scrutinizing the doctor's traumatized face and looked deeply into his eyes. What was he actually saying? The reporter didn't believe the hospital's official statement— that the deceased doctor had been emotionally unstable and took her own life due to her overwhelming stress from the numbers of patients, and even hinted at whether she'd been forced out of the window. The doctor's expression spoke volumes in confirming the reporter's suspicions.

The doctor spoke slowly, choosing his words carefully as he explained how well he knew his colleague and that he couldn't believe she would commit suicide. Then, he courageously surmised, "If she had experienced an emotional break, it was caused by the impossibility of managing the overwhelming number of patients they were receiving daily who were critically ill and dying."

He described the needless loss of so many lives as "excruciatingly painful." Looking down, he added that doctors were "compelled to determine which patient would receive a respirator and have a better chance to survive, and who would be left to end-of-life-care." Lifting his eyes to look directly into the camera, he pleaded for donations of ventilators and protective clothing to help them care for their patients.

If this virus ever reached us, how would I protect Chris? In an instant I went from curiosity and sadness for the world's pain, to drowning under a wave of dread and anxiety over my own family's safety, especially Chris'. The reality of it all crashed into my mind and consumed me. It felt like I was wearing a tight, heavy coat I couldn't take off. I began to sweat, and it was hard to breathe. I had never experienced such high anxiety before, but felt it increase, along with my body temperature.

I couldn't imagine living without my son. Tears filled my eyes as I turned and walked slowly out of my room, hoping to escape my worries. Through blurred vision I looked at my feet which felt heavy and sluggish but were intuitively walking me in slow motion to Chris who was watching a movie in the living room, seemingly without a care in the world. I placed my hand on his shoulder and drew in a much-needed slow breath to shake off the debilitating fears.

Chris saw my tears, grabbed a tissue from the box on the end table and wiped my cheeks.

"OK?" (which I know meant, "Hey Mom, don't be sad. I'm right here. Everything's going to be OK.") He has such a way with words.

"I'm fine, Buddy," I said, just above a whisper. "I'm just thinking about what a hero you are in my world." What I didn't say was, "I'm worried because I don't think I can live without you." I couldn't bring myself to explain what was really going on, but I knew deep in my heart that it was bad.

Chris graciously nodded in agreement, stood up and leaned in for a healing hug. He patted my back until my tears ebbed. I forced them back, looked in his eyes and smiled with feigned happiness.

"Everything will be OK." I assured him. It just had to be.

CoVid wasn't my only fear about Chris' health, his life and his future, and definitely wasn't my first. I knew, logically, that I shouldn't have been so afraid. Chris wasn't. Not because he didn't understand the seriousness of the threatening disease, but because of the way he views the world. He lives simply and peacefully in the present and appears to accept the world as it is. He's been trying to teach me how to have this "it is what it is" attitude his entire life.

Chris doesn't see through any filters of fear and operates on a "what do I want to do" basis. His life has been a continual lesson of the value of removing the filter of debilitating fears from my sight. I remembered those powerful learning experiences I've had throughout Chris' life which helped to dispel many unfounded fears I'd had about raising a child with Down syndrome.

I had suffered too much and far too long through Chris' early childhood when I had allowed unfounded fears to rule my thoughts about the quality of Chris' future life. When living in the present and experiencing the realities of each day, I didn't find cause to worry as much.

Truth is, there's been nothing "Down" about our quality of life and increased happiness with him. In fact, old beliefs about the quality of life for people with Down syndrome were famously debunked by a 2011 Harvard study which found that 99 percent of individuals with this diagnosis were happy with their lives, and 97 percent of their parents and 94 percent of their siblings reported feelings of pride.[4]

But in the year 2020 everything was different.

My fears seemed justifiably based on the catastrophic worldwide pandemic. Government and health care systems were clearly not controlling the spread of the virus

---

[4] Skotko BG, Levine SP, Goldstein R. *Self-perceptions from People with Down Syndrome*. 2011. American Journal of Medical Genetics Part A Volume 155:2360–2369.

and saving enough lives. My fears rocketed to a worst-case scenario: if Chris caught this nightmare virus and I took him to an overcrowded emergency room, would the medical staff take one look at his obvious Down syndrome features and judge him to be the last person in the ER to get a ventilator?

I shared my concerns with friends and family. Many continued to think I was overreacting. Their assurances that things could never get that bad in America didn't console me. Words were inadequate to talk me down from what felt like a narrow ledge.

Because Chris was predisposed to catching pneumonia easily and his history of having a prolonged recovery, I needed a plan of action. Although a lack of medical supplies or appropriate medical care, including the lack of ventilators, happening in America seemed more like a Hollywood horror script rather than a real situation, it was absolutely real in Russia, Italy, and China. And early news reports hinted at similar reports coming from many countries all over the world.

It wasn't long before the pandemic did, in fact, spread to America, and my speculative paranoia became tangible dread. Nationwide news began reporting on our country's lack of medical supplies, including ventilators. For days I thought of nothing else but how I could ensure Chris would get a respirator if he caught the virus and had difficulties breathing. I considered buying a medical ventilator online, but the cost was too high, and I thought it'd be difficult to force a hospital to use my personal medical equipment.

Each passing day brought gloomier news about US hospitals scrambling to acquire supplies and companies struggling to fulfill demands by producing more ventilators. When visualizing the catastrophic future of taking my ill son to a hospital with breathing difficulties, I could foresee staff saying nothing directly to me, but quietly having us linger in the ER waiting room until Chris would be the last patient to be treated. I feared he might not last long enough. Without other reasonable options, I resolved to be ready to file an injunction in court, if needed, for a court to order our local hospital to give Chris proper medical treatment, including a ventilator.

My son deserved a fair chance to survive.

I relied on my legal training in drafting a brief arguing my son's right for an equal opportunity to receive a ventilator. I researched whether any applicable governmental or medical policies during large scale public health emergencies were already in place and found a document published by the US Centers for Disease Control and Prevention (CDC) in July 2011 which appeared to be right on point. It was titled *"Ethical Considerations for Decision Making Regarding Allocation of Mechanical Ventilators during a Severe Influenza Pandemic or Other Public Health Emergency."* The article detailed the need for policies to determine who should be allocated ventilators during a viral disease emergency impacting a large percentage of the population. Although

I accepted the legitimate public purpose for a fair and equitable way to allocate medical equipment when patients outnumber available resources, the more I read, the more pessimistic I became for my son's safety.

The CDC policy addressed the very same scenario posed by the current pandemic citing its own 2007 publication titled, *"Ethical Guidelines in Pandemic Influenza."* My eyes froze on the words in the report, "A public health emergency creates a need to transition from individual patient-focused clinical care to a population-oriented public health approach intended to provide the best possible outcomes for a large cohort of critical care patients." I read that statement over and over, trying to think of a way to debunk it.

I understood that, in normal times, the usual "sickest first" principle is used to triage patients, but in public emergencies government leaders or hospitals could decide to change to a "public benefit" approach. Did this mean patients who "benefit the public" more should have priority to receive a ventilator? How is "benefit to society" appropriately determined? I shuddered as I thought how unfair it would be to Chris—or me—if a government or a hospital leader, ignorant of Chris' value, could take one look at my son and render judgment on whether his life benefits the public enough to qualify for a ventilator.

If Chris caught this highly contagious virus, how would I prove his value? (That Eagle Scout award sure could have come in handy right about now.) The uneasy feeling in my gut turned sour as I further read, "...when resources are scarce, they [policy makers or medical experts] may need to choose to give priority to those who are most likely to recover after receiving them." This meant that decisions for treatment would be like battle-field medical triage when priority is allotted to wounded patients who are most likely to survive, easier to treat with fewer medical resources and have fewer health complications.

Not all people with Down syndrome are equally impacted by a seriously compromised immune system as Chris has been. Throughout his life, he routinely became sicker than anyone in the family when hit by a virus. And he needed more time to recover and required supplemental medications, herbs and vitamins. Chris had been hospitalized several times for pneumonia from a seasonal cold other family members fought off handily. If he were evaluated for ventilator priority, his weakened immune system, along with his extra weight might lead doctors to determine these co-occurring health complications to reduce Chris' likeliness to survive the virus.

The probability of Chris being considered as a higher medical risk motivated me further to be prepared to fight for him to get priority medical care. Apparently, according to what I had been reading, without being deemed to have a life that benefits society, my son could absolutely land at the bottom of the priority list to receive a ventilator.

I had no faith in the government, the public, or medical experts to comprehend the true worth of my son's life.

Consequently, I was in constant fear. I prepared a petition and drafted arguments to obtain judicial intervention, just in case. Even if I were too late to save my son's life, perhaps I could defend another's.

Evidencing Chris' value to society appeared to be a much more challenging task than overcoming the public policy issue. "Because I love my son and can't live without him," would clearly not be persuasive enough of an argument to deem his life a "benefit to the public." It would probably only land me on a suicide watch.

The first perception I needed to tackle—the elephant in the room—was how the world generally misunder-stands Down syndrome. The common stigmatization of it includes archaic, false or incomplete information. I've heard current stories about expectant parents who, upon receiving news of this medical diagnosis, decide to terminate the pregnancy or place their baby for adoption. Perhaps these parents are confused or afraid of the unknown; perhaps they have been told disturbing expectations for their child's quality of life or they fear not being able to handle the diagnosis. I've been there.

Ohhhh, they don't know... I console myself when hearing these types of stories. I mourn with parents who grieve the potential loss of their expectations and dreams. However, I pose a foundational question to these dis-tressed parents, and to everyone—while also challenging it. Should it be considered a burdensome life sentence to have a child with Down syndrome? This existential question elicits our deepest attitudes about the value of every distinct human life.

I wish I could explain to any anguished parents, and the entire world, the good news of the joyful, comforting and life-changing experiences I've had because of my son's diagnosis. Yes, I've lost my own expectations for who my first son may have become, but I've gained so much more. If these parents could spend time with Chris, they'd see how loving, empathic and enjoyable he is. They'd see firsthand how his influence blossomed my life into something better than I—or anyone else—expected.

I believe most people who have family members with Down syndrome feel the same way. Sometimes, when I pass someone else who is accompanying a person with Trisomy 21, our eyes meet, and we share an understanding smile or a knowing wink—an acknowledgment of our mutual good fortune.

For most of Chris' life, I've wanted to shout from the rooftops about the great worth of my amazing son. I've wondered how to explain the many transformative experiences from the lessons he's taught me. The challenge—more than daunting—has seemed impossible. How can I enlighten the world about my son's positive value with my lone voice?

Since the explosion of social media, testimonials have ameliorated many incorrect stereotypes about Down syndrome. Young families across the globe are sharing happy and joyful truths, together with any challenges faced from loving and serving those with this syndrome. One reality that needs to be shared is that the diagnosis, by itself, should not be considered tragic. (But caveat, remember that just like everyone else, no two people with Down syndrome are exactly alike.)

The numerous positive posts on social media affirm the extraordinary influence our family members with Down syndrome have on the world. However, prenatal screening policies in some countries still recommend abortion when this syndrome is detected. Still today, the vast majority of mothers in Iceland who receive a positive test continue to terminate their pregnancy, and the country has infamously boasted to be "almost Down syndrome free." I am so sorry for the people in this region as well as other European countries where the estimated average for abortion was 54% whenever Down syndrome was diagnosed. (Abortion rates were estimated at 50% in Germany, 68% in France and 83% in Spain, compared to 33% in America when Trisomy 21 is detected, according to a 2021 report by AllianceVita.org).

Even among kind and accepting company, when I proudly talk about my son, some are skeptical about my upbeat attitude. Many are silent and seem unsure of what to say—as if we were talking about a funeral. "Is he going to get better?" my mother once asked me. And I've heard several variations of, "he seems to be doing well," but I knew they meant to add, "…considering his diagnosis."

Perhaps I've been judged naïve or unreasonably idealistic, but I've been on this road for forty-five years. I am not whistling in the dark or pretending to be happy. I'm not afraid to face reality about my son's life. Indeed, the truth of being a mother of a son with Down syndrome has formed wings on my heart and my life has taken flight. My biggest fear has since become whether I can live without him.

The joy I've experienced with Chris has surpassed all my hopes and expectations for happiness in motherhood. For this reason, it has been my great pleasure to have shared my son's teachings.

This book has allowed me to explain through life experiences how extraordinarily valuable Chris' life is — not only to me and our family, but to everyone lucky enough to have known him (including all his friends at the gym whom I've never met). His gifts to the world are his teachings which pertain to some of society's greatest needs: unconditional love, understanding, acceptance and happiness.

Without many words, Professor Higgins intuitively understands things and connects with people at a soul level. Although he is slow to speak and his words can sound garbled, his quiet but profound empathy and unconditional love can lift all who truly see him and are influenced by him.

Professor Higgins' life and teachings demonstrate his value in the world and unequivocally evidence his worthiness to receive a ventilator. Every person's life has a distinct and incalculable value, or our human existence has no real meaning at all.

I rest my case.

LESSON 24
Hopefully, this is not... The End

Last Christmas Eve, after tucking my son into bed, I turned off the light in his room and closed the door. For over forty years, he's helped me set out milk and cookies for Santa Claus and carrots for his reindeer. It was only the two of us together that night; his five siblings had long since moved away, and now were tucking in their own children with a reminder to stay in bed for Santa to come. I leaned against the wall recalling times I wasn't as accepting of Chris' forever childhood infatuation with Santa and tried to shrug off self-criticism which crept into my mind bringing discouragement. A feeling of thankfulness for the different lessons Chris taught me flooded over me—especially about being on Team Santa—and subdued my pestering negative thoughts. Again, I was reminded how lucky I have been to enjoy his Christmas Eve happiness for so many years.

Somehow, that Christmas Eve felt more magical than usual. As I pulled out well-hidden gifts to fill my son's

Christmas stocking, I became lost in thoughts of favorite memories from earlier Christmases when my home was full of children. My mind wandered to holidays spent with my own parents—simpler days before I had kids. Those were the stress-free days when I had no idea how much I didn't know about being a parent—when I had innocently, or arrogantly, thought it would be fun and easy to be a mother and how great I would probably be at it! My life certainly didn't turn out anywhere close to what I'd expected when I was a young woman.

In reflection, I could see that twenty-one-year-old mother sitting in the doctor's office hearing the diagnosis of Down syndrome for her precious new baby. I remembered how stupefied and defiant my younger self's reaction was and saw again the sadness in her eyes. I will forever be grateful she was wise enough to ignore the doctor's suggestion to place Chris in an institution. How different and empty my life and our family life would've been!

I wish I could spend a few minutes talking with that young mother to assure her how well everything would work out. My words would've soothed her worries and validated her instinct to trust her intuition when interacting with doctors, other medical experts, therapists or teachers. I'd have counseled her to stay open to their advice and feedback, but to remain confident to venture outside of their proverbial boxes in deciding what is best for Chris.

I wish I could describe to her the quirky experiences and the constant flow of laughter she'll enjoy as she learns about patience—over and over—and to encourage her to be gracious when friends or her mother express sympathy or ask if Chris will get better or "can he be cured?" I'd counsel her about accepting their concerns with love, rather than indignantly thinking, *"Get better? Why? Is he not good enough for you, just the way he is?"*

I'd urge her to avoid judging herself or others too harshly because everyone is usually doing the best they can with what they've got—the information they've got, the experiences they've got, the fears they've got, and the cumulative life challenges they've got. Since pride and judgment can cause negative feelings which close off the heart, I'd also tell her to count on the inspiration she will surely receive as her heart stays open.

The scene in my mind forwarded to that bubbly, over-achieving, head-in-the-clouds, determined young woman marching forward through her twenties to conquer life with a concrete plan to raise up her child to become a man with notable success, regardless of his Down syndrome diagnosis. She sincerely believed her determination and strength would sculpt all her children to accomplish many things beyond their normal expectations. A laugh of delight escaped me as I thought about announcing how the opposite would happen—they, in fact, would change her—and she'd be happier than she could've imagined.

"Chris is a gift for you," I told my younger self. *"He will do more to teach and sculpt you in becoming a better woman, than you will do to mold him."* She wouldn't have believed me. She wasn't quite ready.

Although she'd have initially struggled to understand—because it will take her a few experiences to get comfortable leaning into unfamiliar challenges—I'd love to explain how much happiness can be found in unexpected paths and not to be overly invested in predetermined outcomes. Of course, there'll be many times when she won't know exactly what to expect of Chris, how much to stretch him for improvement and when to accept him as he is. I would explain to her, even at sixty-five years old, I still don't know these answers as they apply to any of my children. But I do know that these issues must be an integral part of the journey of parenthood.

And I could assure my young self that riding the wave of motherhood is much more enjoyable when staying curious about possibilities, and honoring each child's choices, rather than needing to be right and reaching every goal on schedule.

Finally, I wish I could assure Chris' young mother how happy moments will exceed sad ones, that happiness can co-exist with grim times and there can be positive potential outcomes from challenging times. Rather than fearing heartbreak, I'd encourage her to embrace pain and sadness by leaning in and choosing to be broken open— rather than broken down. An open heart is fertile ground for growth and transformation.

Feeling gratitude for the changes I've made through lessons received from my beloved son, Professor Higgins, pulled my thoughts back to the present.

I opened Chris' door a couple of inches to get one more look at my son and noticed he was still awake. I assured him he was on Santa's good list yet again but reminded him he needed to be asleep. He blew me a kiss which soothed my soul and vanquished any lingering self-doubts. A warm wave of peace washed over me watching him snuggle deeper into his sheets.

I walked over and sat in front of the fire becoming cognizant of the blissful smile on my face. It was sweet to realize how much better my life had turned out than I had ever expected. I *had* done some things right when raising my son, particularly in opening my heart to different perspectives and Chris' teachings. Those preliminary lessons of letting go of some expectations, accepting Chris on his terms and surrendering at appropriate times were essential for my ability to embrace change as unexpected lessons continued to reveal themselves.

After sixty-five, I have found myself in another unfamiliar season of life with my son. He is voicing a desire for independence in some ways, including where he lives. When I moved out of state a few years ago, he chose to stay in California and live with his sister and brother-in-law. Chris is thriving with his new freedom and appears happy. I'm the one struggling to be happy while living apart. Although sad to be away from him, I am practicing what my Professor Higgins has taught me over and over— how heartbreak can open me to see and receive new possibilities. Through this perspective, I no longer resent his choice.

The lessons I've learned are more easily recognizable to the woman I am now than to the woman I'd once been. Although I continue to grapple with "knowing when to hold 'em and when to fold 'em" in standing up to my son's desires or societal norms, I look forward to my future journey with more peace than trepidation and more happiness than fear as I continue to explore new possibilities.

Throughout the ride, I hope to never stop enjoying the education offered by my dear Professor Higgins.